MEN OF FAITH IN THE SECOND WORLD WAR

Books by Charles Fraser-Smith

The Secret War of Charles Fraser-Smith.	(£3.50. p & p 80p)
Secret Warriors.	(£2.50. p & p 80p)
Men of Faith in World War II.	(£2.50. p & p 80p)
Four Thousand Year War.	(£3.20. p & p 80p)
The Man Who Was 'Q'.	(£3.95. p & p 80p)

Any five copies post free
All Books obtainable, autographed, from:

Charles Fraser-Smith,
Dale Cottage,
Bratton Fleming,
Barnstaple,
Devon EX31 4SA

MEN OF FAITH
IN THE
SECOND WORLD WAR

Charles Fraser-Smith

The Paternoster Press

British Library Cataloguing in Publication Data

Fraser-Smith, Charles,
    Men of faith in the Second World War.
    1. World War, 1939–1945—Religious aspects
    2. Experience (Religion)—History—
    20th century
    I. Title
    248.2 D744.4

    ISBN 0–85364–453–5

Typeset by Photoprint, Torquay, Devon
and Printed in Great Britain for the Author
by Cox & Wyman Ltd., Reading.

Contents

1

The Secret Services and the Forces

My work in supplying the Secret Service departments of MI6, MI9, OSS, SOE and SAS, in the Second World War, gave me a singular opportunity for seeing faith in action both among members of the forces and among civilians.

My office was adjacent to the headquarters of MI6 in London. What a city that was to be in throughout the War! It became the hub and nerve centre of the world. For it was Britain alone, practically unarmed, that dared to face the evil and aggressive might of Germany which had enslaved the people of western Europe. As the rest of the world watched, the seemingly impossible happened; little Britain resisted. It was her faith which stirred men and women throughout the world.

I saw this faith, not only in members of the three services, but among secret agents and also in government departments. I myself was ostensibly an ordinary civil servant attached to the Ministry of Supply. This proved a unique cover for my clandestine warfare in supplying tools for the job.

Many of the materials used and the gadgets which were thought out, manufactured and delivered, were for various highly secret and often sensitive projects designed to out-fox the enemy. It is rightly said that the victor in war is he who is best informed and prepared. In this war our Secret Services proved that they were the sinews of modern strategic warfare.

Without the intelligence supplied by our MI6 and SOE agents, the generals, Air Force marshals and admirals would not have got very far.

At the centre of our Secret Intelligence was a white-haired, elderly man with pebble glasses, who looked like a retired bank manager. He assumed various names and even personalities. Except for his official passport photograph he never allowed himself to be photographed, even at his wedding. In fact, after his death in 1947, several passports in different names were found at his home at Bathampton Manor, near Bath. He was generally known as Uncle Claude but his full name was Lieutenant Colonel Sir Claude Edward Marjoribanks Dansey, K.C.M.G., C.M.G. He also held the highest honours of France, Belgium, and the United States of America.

Dansey was the most important and influential person in our espionage service and Secret Intelligence before and during the war. He was an elusive person; very little is known about him, as he avoided all paper work, leaving himself free to be continually on the move. Dansey involved himself in just about every aspect of intelligence work. He even kept an eye on my 'innocent job' tucked away in Portland House, a Ministry of Supply building near to his Headquarters in the requisitioned building of Minimax Fire Extinguisher Company, 54 Broadway, opposite St. James Park Underground Station. In 1944, the Broadway buildings were officially placarded as 'Government Communications'.

One day Dansey sent his personal chauffeur, Peggy Van Leer, to take me on a special job. She later married Jimmy Langley, one of my MI9 contacts who, with Airey Neave, had set up escape routes which brought back 3,000 men who had evaded or escaped capture, to fight another day.

Shortly after that I met Dansey for the first and only time, and even then he assumed the identity of one of his men with whom I had often spoken on the telephone, but whom I never met during the war or afterwards. It was understood that his personnel and mine were to avoid meeting as far as was humanly possible and, in order to maintain secrecy, were in no circumstances to enter each other's buildings. The anonymity of everything connected with this job was superb. All orders came over the phone. I never received a written communication, or sent one, in connection with MI6 or with the other secret sections. My own direct chief, G. Ritchie Rice, a director in the Ministry of Supply, knew literally nothing about the work I was doing, except that I was concerned with helping to supply comforts to POWs and even supplying them with escape gadgets – a fairly innocent occupation. He was totally surprised when I sent him my first book revealing the extent of my work.

Even the chief of MI6, Colonel Stewart Menzies, who succeeded Admiral Sir Hugh 'Quex' Sinclair in 1940, was apparently unaware of my work and secret connections. It was not necessary for us to meet and we did not do so. Menzies was quite content to be the figurehead only of MI6. He had some experience of espionage but compared to that of Dansey it was very little.

In fact, while Dansey was on espionage missions in Morocco, Mexico and other places, Menzies, as a young man, was commander of the Regalia Escort of the Crown Jewels, riding beside the king on ceremonial occasions. So he was perfectly willing for Dansey, as Britain's super spymaster, to have practical control of our Secret Services.

This situation suited both men. Menzies was an

adept politician who gloried in the position of offical chief, whereas Dansey preferred to remain anonymous and to be the real – and hidden – power. It also meant that he could get on with his job without the enemy knowing his movements and without anyone bothering him with the minutiae of officialdom. MI6 had been set up to deal with all intelligence matters. There is no doubt that the brain behind it was Dansey who was involved with many, if not most, of the great events of World War II. We shall never know what we really owe to him for our victory, as so far as is known, he kept no records. In fact, he had no time to do so as he was always on the move, using other offices in various secret service buildings and meeting agents in different flats he kept as 'safe houses'.

One advantage of my attachment to the MOS was that the Ministry had taken over complete control of raw materials. That meant that I, as an MOS official, had unhindered use of this material for the making of secret gadgets. At the same time it provided cover for MI6's own top secret workshops where microdots, bugging devices, and other highly sophisticated items and weaponry were handled.

This book has not been written, however, to consider the men in our Secret Departments, but to look at certain men of faith raised up by God to fill key positions in order to deliver us from an aggressive warmonger. Such men were able to use the intelligence supplied and, in some cases, to supply intelligence.

May their undaunted faith challenge us and future generations to follow in their footsteps, for their faith, dedication and courage can never be outdated. May the lives and exploits of these men inspire and encourage us in our daily lives.

I trust I have not been guilty of over-criticism at

times. Destructive criticism is valueless, but factual, constructive criticism can prove invaluable both to the critic and the criticized. Anyone drawing attention to our shortcomings is a true friend. Such criticism helps us to avoid future mistakes. Three thousand years ago Solomon wrote, 'Faithful are the wounds of a friend.'

Many other people could have been included in this book but I have kept to those with whom I was connected or in whom I had a special interest on account of my specific wartime work which can be read about in *The Secret War of Charles Fraser-Smith*,[1] and in *Secret Warriors, the Hidden Heroes of MI6, MI9, OSS, SOE & SAS*.[2]

[1] London, Michael Joseph, 1981, 1983 (available from The Paternoster Press).
[2] Exeter, The Paternoster Press, 1984.

2

Major-General Orde Charles Wingate and the Chindits

The name 'Chindits' comes from the Burmese *chinthe* – a mythical beast that guards the pagodas to ward off evil spirits. It was the name given to the men who took part in Orde Wingate's Long Range Penetration Operations behind the Japanese lines in Burma.

Orde Charles Wingate, the founder of the Chindits, came from an evangelical Christian background; his father, Colonel George Wingate, became a Christian at the age of seventeen. Although brought up in the Church of England, he later joined the Christian Brethren. He also served on the committee of the North Africa Mission, a society with which I myself have had very close contact for sixty years, particularly in their work among Muslims.

After an undistinguished school career at Charterhouse, Wingate joined the Royal Military Academy at Woolwich when he was eighteen. There he gained a reputation for an unconventional attitude towards many of the accepted customs and for his rebellion against the tyranny of dull-minded leaders. He also won respect for his courage and his powers of leadership, which were especially evident in difficult situations.

From Woolwich he was posted to the Sudan, where his progressive outlook and the extremes to which he was prepared to go in desert exercises in order to test his own endurance, proved a trial to his senior officers.

In 1936 he went to Palestine as a member of the Intelligence Service. This posting proved to be the turning point of his life. At first, like most of his army colleagues, he was pro-Arab. Later, however, when the Arabs raised riots in Palestine and persistently damaged the Iraq Petroleum Company's pipe-line (a life-line of the British Empire) causing heavy losses, Wingate began to change his views.

Having learned Hebrew as well as Arabic, he studied the Old Testament to gain an insight into the Jewish character and became intensely interested in the Israeli people. He visited the areas being developed and came to the opinion that the Jews were doing a fine job. He began to make friends with the leading Jews – Dr. Weizmann, Ben Gurion and others. In 1937 he drew up a document which demonstrated a thorough grasp of the situation.

He wrote to Dr. Weizmann, advocating the need for a Jewish Palestine Force, with some British officers included, similar to the Arab Legion in Jordan.

The opportunity to form such a force arose when Sir Archibald Wavell became Commander in Palestine at the end of 1937. He noticed Wingate's unconventional methods and began to consider how his energies and gifts could best be used. As a result, Wingate obtained permission to set up a military intelligence system among Jewish settlements, so that they could defend themselves against Arab raiders, and so that law and order could be established in the north of Palestine. But he came to realize that a defensive strategy was inadequate. Instead the headquarters of the raiders should be secretly sought out and then eliminated. After reconnoitring on his own, he obtained permission to carry out his proposal. It proved successful, and from then on he trained special patrols for the job. They were known as SNS – Special Night Squads.

Wingate set up his HQ at a settlement called El Harod. Because of his knowledge of the Old Testament, it was a place of special interest to him. It was here that around 1249 BC Gideon chose his army to defeat the Midianites. At this spring he watched to see how his men drank. Those who bent double and lapped, regardless of the fact that the enemy might be approaching, he rejected. Those who remained alert and watchful as they drank, scooping up the water in their hands, he retained – some three hundred out of thousands. With this small, specialized unit and an unusual method of surprise night attack, Gideon put a great army of Midianites to flight. The story of Gideon, as told in Judges, was to be an inspiration to Wingate later in his Ethiopia campaign.

His methods gradually became recognized by the British High Command and by leading Zionists. The SNS squads increased and Wingate lectured the recruits on the nature of secret war and leadership. He ensured that they had a unified command, élite manpower and plenty of the right weapons.

He also impressed everyone with his knowledge of Palestine; and whenever he drove about the land he spoke to those who travelled with him about the biblical significance of the places they passed.

The success of his methods made him a legendary character, and his ingenious exploits were a favourite topic of conversation. By organizing these fighting patrols of young Jews he laid the foundation of the Israeli army which was essential for the creation and establishment of Israel as a nation, in the land which God had promised to their ancestor Abraham.

Later, the British Commando and SAS units were also developed from Wingate's squads.

However, when Wingate made it clear that his purpose was to create a Jewish force so that the Jews could defend themselves as a nation, he was recalled to London in 1939. But Churchill was impressed by his summing up of the Palestine problem, and by the SNS units he had set up. Churchill had the foresight to retain Wingate in England in view of the growing threat of a second World War.

When it was finally realized that Wingate's proposal to form a Jewish free army was sound, it was too late for him to return to Palestine. Italy who had invaded Ethiopia in 1935 had now come into the war in Europe, and Wingate was appointed to harass the enemy with guerilla operatives.

In Ethiopia Wingate formed small forces and kept up continual night attacks from different angles, convincing the Italians that he had large forces at his command. Fighting an enemy often twenty times the size of his own army, he forced them to withdraw in fear of being surrounded and cut off.

He found that a small group of ten men, operating at night, was worth twice or even three times that number fighting by day. Not only could an attack be made from several angles, but the silence and suddenness of the approach always proved far more effective. In this, he followed the strategy of Gideon with his night attack on the Midianites – in fact, Wingate's small army was known as 'The Gideon Force'.

He was a man of resilience and endless energy. Hampered by untrained men, poor equipment, totally inadequate transport and no air-support, he still achieved wonders by his military brilliance.

The state entry into Addis Ababa was led by

Wingate on 5 May, exactly five years after the Italian army had entered the capital. His own campaign had been completed in five months. Wingate received orders to go to Cairo, but first he presented himself to the Emperor, Haile Selassie, to say good-bye. The Emperor showed great gratitude and a complete awareness of what Wingate had done for Ethiopia. With his unorthodox methods and his 'Gideon Force' he had enabled the Emperor to enter his capital far earlier than had been thought possible.

When he arrived in Cairo, however, he was relegated to a background role. But he met Oliver Lyttleton, Minister of State, who took the matter up with Churchill. As a result Wingate was brought to London. While he was there, Sir Archibald Wavell signalled the War Office for Wingate to be sent to Rangoon. When other departments heard about the interest in Wingate they woke up and also wanted his services; but it was too late.

Wingate flew to Burma to start guerilla operations. The situation was chaotic; the Japanese were gaining control. The British soldiers quickly recognized Wingate's ability. In due course he had assembled a well-trained fighting force.

Then followed his first Chindit campaign of the rivers Chindwin and Irrawaddy, which caused great confusion to the Japanese. By cutting enemy lines of communication and blowing up dumps he created shortages. His most outstanding success was the continual breaching of the Mandalay-Myitkyina railway, producing disruption of vital supplies to the Japanese forces.

When Wingate's forces returned to the Indian border and HQ, the press took up the story. The fame of the Chindit campaign spread world-wide – the only British success in the Far East up to that time – it may not have been a great military victory, but it proved a great psychological boost. The British soldiers had come to believe that the Japanese were invincible, and this had seriously affected their morale. The success of Wingate's Chindit campaign put new heart into them. It also raised civilian morale at home, where his military operations were talked of everywhere. He had become the symbol of a new hope.

All this had been done in spite of opponents who belittled his achievements and who prevented essential supplies from reaching him.

Wingate had developed his system of irregular warfare in Palestine and East Africa. He had met with success there, and he believed that the stalemate in the wild and inaccessible country of Burma could be broken by operating in strength deep behind the enemy's lines. Unfortunately there were not the resources to prove this, but the stupendous efforts made by the small forces he was able to muster proved to the Japanese that to defend a large jungle front was an impossible task. Such a defence meant over-deployment of their forces, thus weakening both their attack and defence. His long-range penetration plans were excellent; but he was not given the full air-support and wireless facilities which, he insisted, were essential. There is no doubt that unnecessary casualties among his men resulted from lack of air-support. Wounded men, unable to continue, had to be left behind with rations and a revolver, so that they could shoot themselves if necessary.

He also showed wisdom and courage in his opposition to those who wanted to carry on warfare in out-dated, orthodox ways. He threw away all the traditional impedimenta of canvas baths, washstands and other relics of the past which prevented rapid movement. He believed that victory could no longer be obtained by advancing at a leisurely pace, in reasonable comfort, stopping for meals, sleeping in a camp bed or travelling encumbered by a bed-roll.

He insisted that new training was essential to out-think and out-manoeuvre the enemy, and that physical fitness was vital if the Japanese were to be exhausted before our troops were.

Because these new methods were abhorrent to some people's ideas of orthodox military routine, they sought to denigrate him; but at last accurate reports got through to Churchill. He showed his disapproval of the way in which the General Staff had conducted the Far East Campaign, praising Wingate's efforts and calling him the 'Clive of Burma'. In 1943, at an opportune moment, Churchill summoned Wingate home.

After talking to him he wrote, 'I felt myself in the presence of a man of the highest quality . . . . I decided at once to take him with me to the Quadrant Conference.' Before he knew where he was, Wingate found himself travelling on the *Queen Mary* with the Prime Minister and his Chiefs of Staff. At the conference Roosevelt and his Chiefs of Staff were particularly impressed with the results of Wingate's Long Range Penetration methods. In recognition of their faith in him and his plans, an immediate decision was made to provide American soldiers and airmen to support Wingate in forthcoming operations in Burma and the East.

Churchill had no doubts about his personal ability. He wrote, 'I consider Wingate should command the Army in Burma. He is a man of genius and audacity and is a figure quite above ordinary level.'

This decision caused resentment among members of the old conservative military set-up at GHQ, deeply protective of their traditional and comfortable life-style. There was an attempt to ostracise the outsider, and to undermine loyalty to him among his staff and the recruits. Fortunately, many outstanding young men and officers volunteered to join him.

So despite opposition from the establishment, Wingate went ahead. He continued to create original techniques of war, andd he proved that the apparently invincible Japanese army could be defeated. In doing so, he demonstrated the triumph of true character over both British traditionalism and a fanatical enemy. His Chindit campaign was hailed as one of the epics of the Second World War.

The Japanese general Renya Mutaguchi acknowledged that in Wingate he had met his match. Other Japanese commanders also admitted his genius. A document in the National Defence Archives in Tokyo asks, 'What happened in Burma after our triumph? Major-General Orde Wingate, by his methods of guerilla warfare, reduced Japanese ability to wage war in Burma and so fatally affected the balance. In fulfilling this function alone he showed himself a great General.'

Wingate's sudden death at the age of forty-one was tragic. It may itself have been caused partly because of poor air resources. He had repeatedly asked for safer and more suitable aircraft for the job, and it was on returning from a visit to his Chindit troops behind enemy lines that his plane crashed. High Command acted as if he were irreplaceable. They called back his forces and lost some of the great initiative in achieving the rapid conquest which Wingate had envisaged and aimed at. Yet within months of his death, the Japanese defeat was under way.

After the war, efforts were made to denigrate Wingate in order to hide the establishment's failures of strategy; but the Japanese tributes revealed the truth. There is no doubt that Wingate had a difficult temperament and that his personality and achievements will always remain controversial. His near-fanatical dedication brought him enemies. His last remark to his Army Commander before he met his death was, 'You are the only senior officer in South-East Asia who doesn't wish me dead!'

Despite all this those who served under him acknowledged his superb leadership. They recognized too that Wingate's intense concern for them was not the routine care of the ordinary officer. As one of his men said, 'He did not ask for anything but to share the dangers and discomforts of his men.'

Until he spoke or went into action, he was ill at ease. He often made a poor impression. But when he rose to speak, nothing could detract from the force of his words. He inspired men with his own confidence and his troops, the men who had to carry out his plans, were full of admiration for him.

To the Burmese, the name of Wingate was a symbol of protection and deliverance. He risked his life and endured endless hardships to bring them help and freedom. They admired him, not only because of what he did for them, but also because they knew that he understood and genuinely cared for them.

After his death many who had known Wingate paid tribute to him. In the House of Commons, in 1944, Churchhill said:

We placed our hopes at Quebec in the new Supreme Commander, Admiral Mountbatten, and his brilliant lieutenant, Major-General Orde Wingate, who, alas, has paid the soldier's debt. He was a man of genius who might well have become also a man of destiny. He has gone but his spirit lives on in the Long Range Penetration Groups.

Later, in his *History of the Second World War,* Churchill again speaks of Wingate with the same admiration and with personal affection.

At Wingate's memorial service, Leopold Amery spoke of his 'fundamental religious temperament, his capacity for handling men of all races and religions, and his greatness as a leader which lay in qualities beyond mere intellectual grasp. It was of swift daring – it lay in a deep, compelling faith.'

On the memorial tablet to General Wingate in the entrance to the Chapel at Charterhouse School, there is a quotation from Churchill: 'Wingate was one of the most brilliant and courageous figures of World War II.'

Mountbatten said of him:

I had many talks with him and found that he was a remarkable man and that there was a lot to be said for his ideas. Mr Churchill gave him full backing. The Chindits always struck hard, distracting blows at the Japanese and Wingate's men displayed wonderful courage and endurance. After his air-crash I finally pulled his Chindits out. They had done an incredibly dangerous job, and the price concerning their health was high.

There are two other interesting memorials to Wingate. In the hills near Haifa there is a children's settlement named after him – Yemin Orde; he is remembered in Israel with an affection given to no other Englishman except Arthur Balfour. And in Addis Ababa, there is a boys' school named after him.

There is no doubt that Orde Wingate felt that God

had a purpose for him and he always sought to achieve that purpose. He certainly instilled this faith into those around him. Sir Robert Thompson, K.B.E., C.M.G., D.S.O., M.C. – at that time a Flight Lieutenant – writes:

> I do not know of a single man who served under him who would not have gone anywhere with him. Wingate appealed to the spiritual, not the material. We knew that for him, as for Joshua, the walls of Jericho would fall down. I often felt scared but never had any doubts about the success of any operation.

Wingate always carried his pocket Bible with him and quoted from it freely. His words to his men often combined spiritual and practical wisdom. One minute it would be Paul's, 'Quit you like men and be strong' and the next, 'Keep your weapons in perfect condition.' He also knew that in spiritual warfare there is the same insistence on toughness as there is in physical warfare. Paul told Timothy to 'Endure hardship', 'Fight the good fight of faith', 'Be thoroughly equipped', and 'Be fearless'.

The greatness of Wingate's character is seen in the last words that he spoke to his troops before he met his death. 'Finally, knowing the vanity of man's effort and the confusion of his purpose, let us pray that God may accept our services and direct our endeavours so that, when we shall have done all, we shall see the fruits of our labours and be satisfied.'

Week after week, in appalling conditions, Wingate and his men fought against a formidable and ruthless enemy. They fought through jungle and swamp, across raging rivers and in monsoon rain and heat. It is small wonder that no campaign ribbon is worn with greater pride than is the Burma Star.

e.g. P.I.P. FOR A PISTON ; clean it

coat with preservative — to protect preservative,

wrap it — to identify the part, label it

and then put it in a carton — and then label

the carton — to seal up, wrap it

then immerse in a sealing solution — then label

the sealed carton — and then protect the label

so that it will not smudge or peel off

3

Other Aspects of the Burma Campaign

Hugh Seagrim

Another outstanding man in Burma was Hugh Seagrim, an officer in the Burma Rifles. As the Japanese advanced he raised a guerilla force of two hundred Karens which helped to hold them back.

The Karens were believed to have migrated from the borders of China and Tibet. They lived in the hills and had little in common with the other Burmese, having kept their own racial characteristics and language. They made up half of the Burma Rifles. About twenty per cent of them had become Christians through the work of Baptist missionaries. They had always been friendly with British foresters and officials, and had helped in the Burmese campaigns of 1826 and 1852. When the British were expelled from Burma in March 1942, Seagrim decided to remain and live among the Karens.

Living with the Karens, Seagrim prepared for the day when the Allied Forces would return. As he shared their life he became interested in the Christian faith. He read the Bible through and through again. He studied and discussed it with the Karens. Eventually he became a Christian, worshipped with the Karens, and decided that after the war he would devote the rest of his life to helping his Christian Karen friends spread the gospel of Christ amongst the rest of the tribe.

It came to the notice of the Japanese that a British officer was living amongst the Karens. But no Karen would betray him, even under torture, and reprisals began. A Karen who knew Seagrim was captured, and his family seized; he was given a week to find out where Seagrim was and lead them to him, otherwise his whole family would be put to death. On hearing this, Seagrim immediately decided to give himself up to prevent further reprisals. He went to the local Japanese commander, Captain Inove, who sent him to Rangoon where he was held as a prisoner of war. After the war, Inove expressed his admiration for Seagrim.

He also made a lasting impression in the camp. His Japanese guards called him 'Big Master'. A fellow-prisoner, a pilot, said, 'I believe him to be the finest gentleman I have ever met. He had the greatest concern for the Karens and a complete disregard for his own life.' He organized Bible study groups with his fellow prisoners and prayed for the Japanese staff and guards. He was eventually executed by the Japanese, as the hierarchy considered him responsible for the guerilla warfare.

Within a year of his death, Karens who had belonged to the Burma Rifles were armed by means of SOE drops of modern weapons. During 1944 they formed themselves into formidable guerilla groups, achieving effective and very widespread action, which gave invaluable assistance to the British re-conquest of Burma.

Secret Supplies to Burma

I helped to furnish Orde Wingate and his Chindits with special equipment and concentrated rations, and provided secret supplies for our SOE agents in

Burma. I also became involved in another challenging and intriguing task.

Even if they have great commanders and unfailing courage, soldiers lose confidence and suffer devastating set-backs and even loss of lives if equipment arrives damaged or corroded and fails them when it is most needed. This was the cause of much unnecessary loss of life in the jungles of Burma.

Consequently, *tropical packing* of spare parts became a priority matter for that part of the world. This is a side of war that very few have heard about, and yet it is of great interest.

A tank, lorry or gun would break down. A spare part would be brought which had been in store, perhaps only for a few weeks; but when unpacked it would be found to be corroded and useless – and every package to be the same. That tank or other piece of equipment was vital, but it was now useless. And further supplies were in Britain, 6,000 miles away.

What a waste of time and invaluable material this was, and what an advantage it gave to the Japanese!

The temperature could reach 100° in the shade, and 165° in the sun, with an 80 per cent to 90 per cent humidity. This encouraged rapid corrosion and fungoid and bacterial growth. Inches of rain fell in an hour, and in such colossal heat and humidity a packing case became a stewpot and a store tent a Turkish bath. Verdigris formed on brass; aluminium and plastics corroded; steel parts rusted overnight; rubber rotted, and other things decomposed.

Jungle pests also fought in this war of attrition. Ants ate packaging materials; termites bored into rifle stocks; mould spoiled leather goods. Even glass was not immune as bacteria formed on medical and optical instruments, obscuring lenses. The medical needs alone called for a supply of thousands of different items.

So a blitz operation was set up to search for a remedy for this problem. Its success proved invaluable later, when supplying goods to those countries needing rehabilitation after the war.

To prevent the appalling wastage of equipment of every description in the Far East theatre of war and to ensure that soldiers got what they needed in fully usable condition, 'PIP' was inaugurated (P – Preservation of stores; I – Identification of stores; P – Packaging of stores).

We took over the premises of Slazengers Ltd. at Pinder Oaks Works in Barnsley, Yorkshire. We removed their equipment and re-equipped the premises overnight. Slazenger's staff stayed on and organized the operation excellently.

The first step was thorough cleaning. All contaminants on the parts, such as salt residues from perspiration in handling, dust, and general factory and atmospheric impurities had to be removed. Drying by oxygen or compressed air jet followed immediately. (In fact, all the processes formed a single continuous procedure, and there was no pause until the part was packed for shipment. Rubber conveyor belts maintained an even flow.)

The parts were treated with fungicidal and anti-corrosive liquid film preservatives. Care had to be taken that these would not interfere with the usability of the equipment. It was no good preventing corrosion inside a part, if the preservative itself became a solid coating that prevented the engine from working.

The part was then wrapped in special waterproof and pliable packing material which could be moulded to the shape of the part. This was not only to protect it, but also to eliminate air. The less air left in a package, the less chance there was of condensation causing corrosion. In special cases a dessicant was included which absorbed atmospheric moisture. Finally, to make sure that the wrapped part was absolutely waterproof, it was dipped in wax.

Labelling and enclosure in a carton followed. The carton was wrapped in greaseproof paper. Waterproof adhesive was applied and a lock-seam joint formed. The carton was dipped in wax in two stages, first to slightly more than half the depth of the package, and second, by reversing the package, to the remaining half, to produce a one inch overlap of the wax coating. The package was re-identified and the label covered with transparent adhesive waterproof wax, and then stored.

The most interesting step was the final packaging for transport in wooden packing cases. All timber, when felled, contains a large quantity of moisture. Certain soft woods contain moisture to the amount of twice the weight of the wood substance. So the wood used had to be well-seasoned, or kiln dried. Certain woods such as oak and sweet chestnut, because of their acidic properties, which would release acid vapours, could not be used. Unseasoned wood in the tropics can pit machined steel parts and render them useless within forty-eight hours!

After the wood had been seasoned or dried, then treated with a preservative, case liners made from bitumen laminated paper were inserted and the parcels packed in the cases. The case-linings were lock-seamed with adhesive, the lid nailed down and the box wired ready for transport, with non-rusting nails and wire.

Thus MOS, too, played its part in the Burma Campaign!

4

Michel Hollard D.S.C.

General Eisenhower wrote in his book *Crusade in Europe* (1949),

> If the Germans had succeeded in perfecting and using their new weapons, such as the flying bomb (V–1) and later the V–2, six months earlier than they did, our invasion of Europe would have proved exceedingly difficult, perhaps impossible. I feel sure that if they had succeeded in using these weapons over a six month period, and particularly if they had made the Portsmouth/Southampton area one of the principal targets, *Overlord* (D-Day) might have been written off.

Winston Churchill paid his own tribute to the agents and all who risked their lives to save London and the rest of England from the danger of the flying bomb.

> Our Intelligence played a vital part, and every known means of getting information was employed and pieced together with great skill. To all sources, many of whom worked amid deadly danger, and some of whom will be for ever unknown to us, I pay my tribute.

There can be no doubt about the devastation caused by the flying bomb. I remember one falling within a third of a mile of me, killing a hundred people and shattering thousands of windows. They were first launched against England on 14 June 1944, and in only two months damaged over 1,000,000 houses.

The flying bomb attacks were quickly halted by Montgomery's advance north. They had already decreased as a result of the destruction of sites by Bomber Command after information from secret agents, particularly Michel Hollard. Even today it is not generally realized how much we owe to this one man.

When France surrendered, Michel Hollard was a technical representative for a large firm specializing in brake linings. Finding they were switching over to supplying the Germans, he resigned, since he was determined to do nothing to help the enemy. He found it difficult to support his family, as he turned down job after job so as not to violate his principles. Eventually he heard of an engineering firm producing gas engines, run on charcoal, for motor cars. The demand by the French began to grow as petrol supplies became more and more restricted. He acquired the agency for Paris, and with his contacts in the engineering world he was so successful that he was appointed sole concessionaire with powers to appoint his own representatives.

This meant not only that he could travel widely, seeking the wood necessary for making charcoal, but also that he was provided with the ideal cover for clandestine activities to help to rid his country of the German invader.

The headquarters of *Gazogene Autobluc,* of which he became agent-general, were at Dijon, not far from the border with Switzerland. By buying wood along the border he found a way to cross secretly into Switzerland and decided to offer his services to the British Military Attaché in Berne.

After exciting adventures on foot and bicycle, he saw the English major in charge. He was received in a cool, offhand way and given no encouragement.

Although he was annoyed by this reception, Hollard's enthusiasm was not dampened. Indeed, he was satisfied at having achieved two objectives. He had found a way of leaving and re-entering France; and he had made an initial contact with Britain. So he was determined to persevere.

On his return from his first trip to Switzerland, Michel Hollard decided to work independently of all other French and British underground organizations. His was to be a one-man effort, and therein lay its greatest advantage and protection.

He avoided using radio for intelligence transmissions, as the Gestapo could track down agents who were transmitting. Moreover, a man captured with his transmitter could be used by the Germans to lay traps for many other agents. Also, by using a Swiss 'post box', full details with photographs, plans and documents could be sent, which were impossible to transmit by wireless. As time passed he gradually recruited others to help him to collect information until he had over a hundred working for him. But each was unknown to the rest, having contact with Hollard alone. Thus, if one was caught, tortured or questioned, Hollard alone would be betrayed. These contacts met him at regular stated intervals or he met them on his travels for the firm. By this means a vast amount of important information concerning German military movements reached Britain.

In the latter half of 1943 Michel Hollard brought off his greatest coup. Hearing of new and unusual constructions being erected some thirty miles inland from the coast, he decided to investigate for himself. To get into the area he went to the Social Department of the local Labour Office connected with the installations and said he was a Protestant Welfare worker. He showed the contents of his case, which contained moral and religious booklets, such as *The Scourge of Disease, Christian Marriage,* and Bibles. The official thought it an excellent idea for these to be distributed to help these workers so cut off from their families and exposed to grave moral dangers. A permit was granted for him to do social work on these sites.

Hollard, once on the sites, was able to exchange jobs with a workman and soon found that launching ramps were being installed pointing towards London and other important targets. He had one of my miniature cameras with him, and the films he took were hidden in various secret items manufactured for my 'Q' department, such as a shaving brush or dummy torch cells. They were delivered to Switzerland and passed quickly to London. In a few weeks a hundred sites were located and reported. Michel Hollard waited. Were the Allies never going to take action?

On 15 December 1943 they struck. Hollard's location of these sites had been confirmed by aerial photographs interpreted by Constance Babington-Smith of the Photographic Reconnaisance Unit of the RAF. Charles Packard, a brilliant pilot, who had landed and picked up some of our SOE agents in France, was chosen to lead the bombing of the sites.

The modelling section at Medmenham (to whom I supplied the materials) built up a replica site, where Packard and his crew were thoroughly briefed and acquainted with the lay-out of the targets.

The sites were too minute for ordinary bombers to hit with accuracy from a height, so a series of daylight, low-level attacks was started. Forty-eight Mosquitoes flew low over the Channel. They hugged the ground at zero feet to fox the enemy radar. The sites, having been pin-pointed, were then bombed with devastating accuracy, and the fast-moving air-craft were away before the Germans knew what had hit them. The enemy then had to transfer the launching of the flying bombs to big aircraft which acted as mobile launching pads.

Hollard himself personally inspected the bombed sites and so was able to see the results of all the risks he and his friends had taken. The launching of these terrible weapons had been reduced to a minimum.

Suspicion finally fell upon Michel Hollard. Al-though, at first, he was able to get rid of his 'shadow' he was finally, like many others, betrayed into the hands of the Gestapo. For three hours he was put through the 'bath' torture. At last, in exasperation, his torturers concluded, 'We are wasting our time on this man!' So they left him, half-dead, lying on the floor. There an elderly Italian woman, employed in the building, gently fed him. Later, guards took him back to his cell. His modest comment on his resist-ance was, 'God gave me a wonderful deliverance in tiring them before me.'

After a spell of imprisonment he was sent to a forced labour camp. He was put in charge of four machines, turning out breech parts for machine guns. Each day he concealed four parts and disposed of them in the latrine blocks. Every evening, as he passed the guards and searchers, he steeled himself against detection and death. On two hundred and seventy one occasions he risked his life.

As the Allies advanced the Germans decided to liquidate their prisoners in a horrifying way, which typified the Nazi desire for revenge. Prisoners were locked in the holds of old German ships. These were set adrift in the North Sea with engines running, but no crew aboard. When challenged by the Allied aircraft, they were unable to stop or reply and were naturally destroyed. The first two floating coffins, the *Deutschland* and the *Caparcona,* were bombed and sunk and the thousands on board were drowned.

The *Thilboek's* turn came, and when the engines started up Hollard guessed what was in store for them. He raised his voice and, in the darkness, addressed his fellow prisoners: 'My friends, our turn has come to set out. We are all afraid. This is the moment to show what sort of men we are. Some of us are believers, or claim to be. Christ said, "When two or three or more are gathered together in my name there shall I be, and they shall not call on me in vain." We shall now make a chain with our hands and I will pray for help.' Michel lifted up his voice: 'Oh, God, come to our aid. Whatever happens, we beseech you to protect our wives and our children and guard them, in the name of Jesus Christ.'

He had scarcely finished praying when the vibration of the ship's engines ceased. Mercifully a Swedish Red Cross boat had stopped and taken possession of the *Thilboek.*

They were put on two Swedish merchant ships and found themselves in luxury after the awful experience of being locked for days in the stinking hold of the German boat.

When they arrived at a small port, women of the Swedish Red Cross were waiting to receive them. Their clothes were taken away and burnt, and nurses wearing protective clothing, gloves and masks, scrubbed and bathed them.

The day after Michel Hollard's arrival in Sweden, Mme. Hollard received a visit from a high British official informing her that her husband was safe and that he had been awarded the D.S.C., the highest decoration for bravery which Britain can bestow upon a foreigner.

Some weeks later, when he was considered fit enough to travel, a Swedish Red Cross plane flew him and a party of ten others to France. It flew over the V–1 site at Bonnetôt le Faubourg for Michel to see the results of the RAF bombing. To see that mass of rubble and twisted girders from the security of the plane was an unforgettable experience. He had not only recovered his own freedom, but by helping to destroy such devices he had contributed to the defeat of an evil enemy whose aim was world domination.

Soon after his arrival in France an RAF plane arrived to take him to London, where a special reception had been arranged, but for Michel Hollard the climax of the celebrations had been the welcome given to him by his own family.

Both Hollard and his wife were practising Christians and had inherited some of the spiritual determination of their Huguenot ancestors. He had a deep faith in God and in the righteousness of his cause, and wonderful powers of endurance. It is almost incredible to think that he crossed the very heavily guarded frontier between France and Switzerland ninety-eight times, in order to pass on information in person so that it would be completely accurate.

The spiritual motivation behind this determination can be seen in the fact that when he first recrossed the frontier back into France he stopped, not to rest, but to offer thanks to God for his help.

Michel Hollard was a hero of the first order. There are no headlines for the lone secret agent. Too many books and official histories of the Second World War are written by the establishment for the establishment, and make no mention of the agents whose work really won the war. The debt we owe to them can never be over-stated.

5

Field Marshal Viscount Montgomery
K.G., G.C.B., D.S.O.

Field Marshal Montgomery had the following quotation hung on the wall of the caravan which he used as his HQ throughout the Second World War.

> O Lord God, when Thou givest to Thy servant
>   to endeavour any great matter,
> Grant us also to know that it is not the beginning
>   but the continuing of the same
>   until it is thoroughly finished
>   which yieldeth the true glory,
> through Him who for the finishing of Thy work
>   laid down His life – our Redeemer, Jesus Christ.
>   Amen.
>
> (*Prayer of Sir Francis Drake*)

In this prayer we catch a glimpse of Montgomery's basic motivation. It was his deep faith in God and in the teaching of the Bible. He believed that his life was in God's hand. Every day he would take time to think and to read, particularly God's word. He said to the members of his staff: 'Gentlemen, I read my Bible every day and I recommend you to do the same.'

One of his favourite verses was, 'Only be thou strong and very courageous' – the words spoken by God to Joshua when he was appointed by God to lead his people.

In one of his speeches Montgomery challenges us all:

Let us remember, when all things are done, that one great fact remains supreme and unassailable. It is this. There are in this world things that are true and things that are false; there are ways that are right and ways that are wrong; there are men good and men bad. And on one side or the other we must take our stand; one or the other we must serve. A great commander once dismissed his troops with these words, 'Choose this day whom you will serve. As for me and my house we will serve the Lord' [Joshua 24:15]. It is my belief that these words must be impressed on every young person from the earliest days.

He carried this faith in God into all his military activities. He believed that it is only when a commander has a proper sense of Christian truth that he can inspire his men to fight bravely in a righteous cause.

This Christian faith, and many of his personal characteristics, can be traced back to his childhood and later experiences. He was born in 1887, one of a family of nine. He had a deep love and admiration for his father, who at one time was Bishop of Tasmania. Of his mother he himself said:

My mother was a remarkable woman . . . . She taught us to speak the truth and exerted her authority over us. If my strong will had gone unchecked and had not been disciplined, the result might have been even more intolerable than some people found me. It became clear to me that my early troubles were mostly my own fault.

In 1927 he married Betty Carver, and a period of great happiness began. But in 1937 Betty was in India with her husband and their son David when an earthquake struck Quetta. She exhausted herself in her efforts to assist the rescue work, and while her resistance was lowered, sepsis set in after she had received an insect bite. Her leg was amputated, but the poison continued to spread. She died in October 1937. Some of the last words she heard from her husband were those of the Twenty-third Psalm.

Montgomery was shattered by her death, and it was some time before he was able to take up his military duties again. Although he appeared to return to normal life it is probable that had his wife lived he would not have developed many of the 'egocentricities' which annoyed other people.

During his life, and since his death, Montgomery has had many critics. But much of this criticism is unjustified and comes from small-minded people who wish to detract from his undoubted achievements.

Many, for instance, criticized him for what they saw as a lack of modesty. Yet confidence in himself and his men was one factor which contributed to his many victories. He was accused of being too ambitious. But while it is true that he enjoyed leadership, his greatest ambition was to maintain moral principles in his own life and in the lives of those who served under him.

His military tactics have also been questioned. It has been said that he was too cautious. But, as we shall see, it was this caution both in the North Africa campaign and in Europe which saved the lives of so many of his soldiers and helped to increase their confidence in his leadership. Indeed, one of Montgomery's most outstanding attributes was the relationship he established with his own men.

In the First World War he had been struck by the lack of contact between generals and their soldiers. These generals remained in the rear and were unaware of the appalling conditions under which their men were fighting. Montgomery was determined that his own men would feel able to trust him because they were convinced that he had a personal interest in their welfare.

When, in September 1942, he was given command of the Eighth Army in Egypt he quickly built up the morale of his soldiers and soon led them to victory against Rommel and the experienced and well-armed German Korp. His triumph at El Alamein helped to destroy the myth of the invincibility of the German forces. He inspired confidence in the men of the Eighth Army both in their own powers of fighting and in his power to lead them to victory. They felt completely secure under his command.

He himself paid a high tribute to his men.

The British soldier is second to none. In the midst of the noise and confusion of the battle-field, the homely British soldier stands out calm and resolute. His quiet courage, humour and cheerfulness dominates. His greatness is a measure of the greatness of the British character and I have seen the quality of our race proved again and again on the battle-field.

He was concerned too about his men's personal welfare. He saw that a modern commander needs to gain the confidence of his men and to exercise his authority wisely and sensibly. He rejected the attitude which saw an army as just a collection of equipment and men. Nor did he rely solely on amenities such as canteens and NAAFI clubs to maintain morale. Instead he stressed the need for the commander to take personal thought for the good of his men.

When Churchill was inspecting the desert troops he asked Monty, 'What can I do to show my pride in these splendid fighting men?'. Montgomery replied that they would appreciate a quicker postal service, as mail took so long coming round the Cape of Good Hope. So when Churchill returned to England he gave orders for this to be remedied. In the end I myself helped to overcome this problem. I had been handling microfilming for secret work. The process was adapted and microfilm service by air was inaugurated. In proved a great morale booster for the men to receive mail in a week instead of months.

Montgomery's personal interest in his men was shown again when the army, after defeating Rommel at Alamein, had covered 1,200 miles in two months and ensured the safety of Egypt. Montgomery decided that his men deserved a rest and should be given an opportunity to celebrate Christmas. He sent them a personal message, reminding them of what they owed to God for their victories and enclosing a Christmas greeting which had been sent to him by 'a Yorkshire lass with a lad in the Eighth Army'. He also arranged for a supply of turkeys and plum puddings for his men.

After Christmas Montgomery received a letter from an ordinary private soldier.

> There can never have been such a message read to troops before. For the first time in my Army life I felt I belonged. Your man to man message had a tremendous effect on our spirits. You achieved far more by your human, personal approach than any Order of the Day could have done. You have made us proud to belong to the Eighth Army. God bless you, Sir, and guide you at all times.

But it was not only the men involved in the actual fighting who were inspired by Montgomery's trust in them. As well as speaking to over a million members of the fighting forces he also visited and spoke to the factory workers. He pointed out how, to our shame, equipment had been totally inadequate at the beginning of the war. He stressed the need for the very best-made weapons. He emphasized the fact that the efforts of the factory workers were as important as those of his army. Only as workers and soldiers were welded together would we be able to escape German domination. He found many of these factory workers war-weary and these talks inspired them to make the maximum effort in their work.

Montgomery's fighting abilities and leadership also won the admiration of Winston Churchill. He said of Montgomery, 'Before Alamein we never had a victory – after Alamein we never had a defeat.' Churchill took every opportunity to visit Montgomery when he was fighting abroad, and when he was in England often invited him to Chequers. His admiration for Montgomery was such that he was even prepared to accept orders from him. On 19 May 1944 Churchill arrived at Monty's HQ because he was not satisfied about certain arrangements for D-Day. Montgomery took him into his study and straightaway said, 'I understand, Sir, that you want to discuss with my staff the operation. I cannot allow you to do so. My staff advise me on detail and I give the final decision. That final decision has been given. I cannot allow you to harass my staff at this time and possibly shake their confidence in me. You can argue with me, but not with my staff. In any case, it is too late to change anything.'

Montgomery took Churchill into the next room and introduced him to his staff. As Churchill entered he said, with a twinkle in his eye, 'I am not allowed to have any discussion with you gentlemen.' Then they had a most amusing dinner together. Although Churchill accepted this ultimatum, Montgomery often aroused hostility by his uncompromising attitudes, especially to others in authority.

After the defeat at Dunkirk (which he never allowed to be called a victory) Montgomery criticized the lack of modern training and equipment. He himself was anything but a conventional commanding officer. His popularity with staff officers was not increased by his claim that there are no bad regiments – only bad officers. He was determined that all staff, even those engaged on clerical work, should be absolutely fit, and ordered training to be carried out in all weathers.

When he was briefing his officers, nothing was allowed to disturb concentration. Those who arrived late were kept waiting outside until Montgomery had finished dealing with a specific subject. Smoking was discouraged, as he believed that it had a distracting influence.

The climax to Montgomery's fifty years of unbroken service came in the D-Day Campaign.

One problem which Montgomery faced in this campaign was the hostility and criticism of some of the American generals, particularly Patton, who hated Montgomery and constantly tried to thwart him.

The Americans, on the whole, were envious of Montgomery's knowledge and the tactical successes he had achieved through his intelligence officers. Very often they refused to cooperate with these officers, which made it difficult for Montgomery to obtain full information about the US forces under him.

At Omaha Beach the advice provided by our SOE and other intelligence sources was neglected, and the Americans suffered appalling and unnecessary casualties. Montgomery's own planning and execution of the Normandy landing and the vital battles of Caen and Falaise were magnificent. Two months later, on 9 August 1944, Eisenhower landed and took full command; but he lacked experience in the handling of armies and complications arose.

Montgomery's plan was to seize the nearby Channel Ports before they could be destroyed, eliminate the dangerous rocket sites and neutralize the Ruhr which produced Germany's coal and where the factories were sited which were essential for Germany's war. A German general, Blomentritt, has said, 'He who holds the Ruhr holds Germany, and a thrust north by Eisenhower would have torn the German front to pieces and ended the war six months earlier.'

The American generals favoured an Allied advance on a broad front, which Montgomery bluntly forecast would come to a halt through lack of petrol, transport and supplies so that the war would continue into the next year. Despite this warning, Bradley and Patton advanced on several fronts. Eventually logistic support was unable to keep up and the advance had to be halted. Every item had to be transported hundreds of kilometres, by long sea routes to Normandy and from there by land to the fronts.

If the Allied forces had held a short line and concentrated on a thrust north, then our supply lines would have been along tens and not hundreds of kilometres and the war would have ended sooner. When Montgomery captured Antwerp and Brussels and reached Holland on 4 September 1944 he had to halt. There was no petrol and no supplies. They had been used up in the advance to the east far from the great armament production areas of Germany.

The German generals themselves were surprised when Montgomery came to a halt. They agreed that his sudden penetration north and into Antwerp had taken them by surprise, and that if he had been backed by his High Command nothing could have stopped his further advance. They also agreed that

Patton's break-through in the south, their weak spot, was spectacular but not vital to the winning of the war.

When Montgomery reached Antwerp he tried again to persuade the High Command to take advantage of the situation. They failed to do so. Our SOE agents and members of the Dutch Resistance had correctly informed the American High Command of the weak and disorganized state of the German forces, but this information was also disregarded. As a result, the Germans were given time to recover; and there followed the disaster and unnecessary loss of life at Arnhem, and the devastating attack on the Americans in the Ardennes, where they suffered nearly 80,000 casualties. Montgomery was forced to break off his own offensive, losing six important weeks, to come to their rescue. Eisenhower, at least, recognized the importance of this action and later wrote, 'Thank you for the way you pitched in to help during the German thrust at Ardennes.'

On that occasion the Germans had, in fact, copied the tactics Montgomery had used against them at Caen and Falaise. He had kept in check seven German panzer divisions and four heavy tank battalions at Caen so that the Americans could advance. This forced the Germans into a rapid retreat, leaving the bulk of their equipment behind and some 50,000 of their troops trapped.

Another striking contrast between Montgomery and the American military leaders lay in their choice of headquarters. Eisenhower remained in a chateau at Granville, four hundred miles behind the front lines, which often caused delay in the implementing of decisions. The German High Command also used this type of accommodation. When Montgomery realized this he sent out airforces to destroy the buildings at the German HQs. In the battle of

Normandy alone, twenty-two German generals were killed in this way. By contrast, Montgomery had his own HQ in a caravan which could be hidden in an orchard or well camouflaged. It was also easily moved. He was therefore readily available and could quickly be reached for consultations with his commanders and was, in any case, in close field-telephone communication with them.

The crowning climax to Montgomery's long and hard fight from Alamein to Berlin was undoubtedly the signing of the Surrender Document by the German High Command on 4 May 1945. But even then he did not relax his efforts. He immediately began to make efforts on behalf of the prisoners of war, and worked ceaselessly for the welfare of the British army of occupation.

His final message to all troops, issued as the war came to an end, displays the greatness of the man:

21 ARMY **GROUP**

PERSONAL MESSAGE
FROM THE C-IN-C

(To be read out to all Troops)

1. On this day of victory in Europe I feel I would like to speak to all who have served and fought with me during the last few years. What I have to say is very simple, and quite short.

2. I would ask you all to remember those of our comrades who fell in the struggle. They gave their lives that others might have freedom, and no man can do more than that. I believe that He would say to each of them:

    "Well done, thou good and faithful servant."

3. And we who remain have seen the thing through to the end; we all have a feeling of great joy and thankfulness that we have been preserved to see this day.

    We must remember to give the praise and thankfulness where it is due:

    "This is the Lord's doing, and it is marvellous in our eyes."

4. In the early days of this war the British Empire stood alone against the combined might of the axis powers. And during those days we suffered some great disasters; but we stood firm: on the defensive, but striking blows where we could. Later we were joined by Russia and America; and from then onwards the end was in no doubt. Let us never forget what we owe to our Russian and American allies; this great allied team has achieved much in war; may it achieve even more in peace.

5. Without doubt, great problems lie ahead; the world will not recover quickly from the upheaval that has taken place; there is much work for each one of us.

    I would say that we must face up to that work with the same fortitude that we faced up to the worst days of this war. It may be that some difficult times lie ahead for our country, and for each one of us personally. If it happens thus, then our discipline will pull us through; but we must remember that the best discipline implies the subordination of self for the benefit of the community.

6. It has been a privilege and an honour to command this great British Empire team in western Europe. Few commanders can have had such loyal service as you have given me. I thank each one of you from the bottom of my heart.

7. And so let us embark on what lies ahead full of joy and optimism. We have won the German war. Let us now win the peace.

8. Good luck to you all, wherever you may be.

B. L. Montgomery

Field-Marshal,
C.-in-C.,
21 Army Group.

Germany,
May, 1945.

6

Lieutenant-General Sir William George Dobbie, G.C.M.G., K.C.B., D.S.O.

Malta has always been a key to the entire Mediterranean, from the times of the Phoenicians and through those of the Carthaginians, Romans, Arabs and the Knights of the Order of St. John. In 1815 the Maltese, at their own request, became 'subjects of the British Crown and entitled to its fullest protection'.

In the Second World War the island became a great obstacle in the path of Italy and Germany. It impeded supplies to their Northern Africa Campaigns, and that was due to the fact that General Dobbie was made Governor and Commander-in-Chief in April 1940. If Malta had been captured, then supply ships could have made their way unhindered to Tripoli or Benghazi, unescorted and at whatever speed they chose.

When Italy entered the war Germany gave her the job of wiping out Malta. Incredibly, apart from the British naval base, no preparations had been made to defend the island. In this new task the prospects for General Dobbie were far from hopeful. The infantry was not up to full strength, and there were no fighter aircraft to defend the island. It was considered that Malta could not be held if Italy and Germany attacked – it was too vulnerable from the air.

But Dobbie did not intend to die heroically under crushing attacks. Without wasting a moment he immediately broadcast to the people in order to raise morale. He gave them precise instructions on what to do in air raids and asked for volunteers to form a Home Guard. The response was overwhelming. But at the same time he made clear his reliance on God.

A search in the dockyard revealed four Gloster Sea Gladiator fighters in packing cases. The carrier *Glorious* had been forced to leave them behind, with orders for them to be crated and sent to Alexandria. By 'cannibalising' the fourth, three were made ready immediately. Fortunately, some flying-boat pilots and ground staff were on the island, along with mechanics, and they did a magnificent job modernizing these sturdy aircraft, and they quickly learnt to handle them.

Dobbie's Order for the Day was:

> We will fight until our enemies are defeated. All ranks will not falter and with God's help we will maintain the security of this island. I call on all humbly to seek God's help and then, in reliance on Him, to do your duty unflinchingly.

Meanwhile in Italy, Mussolini, the strutting dictator, had made himself Secretary of Air. His pride, the large Fascist Air Force with excellent and fast modern planes based in Sicily, only ten minutes' flying time from Malta, rested confidently, assured of success, awaiting the order to begin an easy task. Mussolini addressed the crowds from his balcony with bombastic rantings: Malta must surrender immediately, or be obliterated. What a contrast to Dobbie's calm trust in God!

The first Italian raid was on 11 June 1940. The large bomber formation was driven off by those three Gladiators! Against overwhelming odds, with maintenance parties working non-stop round the clock, repairing and patching, the three planes together with the anti-aircraft batteries of the naval base, collected a large bag of downed enemy aircraft.

No wonder the people of Malta loved Dobbie and these pilots! The three aircraft were named 'Faith, Hope and Charity'. With their God-fearing General Dobbie, the people certainly had the faith, and for three weeks those old, battered planes were their only hope. They were appropriately named from the thirteenth chapter of Paul's first letter to the Corinthians. 'Faith' was the only one that survived; it stands proudly today in the museum of the Royal Palace of Valetta, a fitting symbol of courage and the will to stand firm whatever the odds.

When the main petrol tank of Peter Hartley's Gladiator was hit by an incendiary shell, the non-self-sealing tank located in front of him deluged him with burning petrol. Crazed with pain, and ignoring the parachute, he went over the side into the sea. A boat picked him up. Staff at the hospital despaired of his life, so a fellow pilot brought along Dobbie's young, attractive daughter. Looking at his heavily bandaged body, she said, 'Hello Peter, I hear you fell out of your aeroplane!' From then on he picked up rapidly. Through courage and persistence he recovered. He was given a desert squadron at Al Alamein, flying 'Tank-Buster Hurricanes' armed with cannon.

Dobbie was an incurable optimist. Although he was kept so busy with the defence of Malta, he was clear-headed enough to see its strategic position as an offensive base, for the attack on enemy shipping to North Africa and the harassing of Axis communications. Malta should be an unsinkable aircraft carrier! He put this idea to Churchill.

On 28 June a raid had just ended. The pilots were having their machines serviced when suddenly there was a roar overhead. Four monoplanes were coming in low. Startled, they took cover; then they looked up and were amazed. The planes were Hurricanes.

As the authorities in England saw that Malta was holding out and could be an unexpected asset under its 'remarkable and resolute governor' (as Churchill described Dobbie), they accepted his assessment of the situation. Hurricanes, Spitfires and other planes were hurried to the island. Reinforcements and guns were also sent. They made possible the resounding success at Taranto and the total crippling of the Italian fleet in November 1940. Dobbie's determination that the island should hit back was fulfilled. Malta went on the offensive in 1941. The toll taken of German convoys to North Africa mounted in June to 7 per cent, in August to 25 per cent, in September to 40 per cent, in October to 63 per cent and in November to 77 per cent. But the greatest moment of all for the Maltese came when the Italian fleet surrendered and lay at anchor under the guns of Malta.

The debt Malta and Britain owe to this great and committed Christian is incalculable. By his personal example and trust in God, he forged a magnificent bond between civilians and service personnel that withstood incredible hardship, hunger, suffering and even death.

Every evening after dinner, all guests were invited to the drawing room and there Dobbie publicly prayed concerning Malta and the war situation as a whole. On his desk, together with his papers, files and telephone, there was always his Bible to which he often referred. On one occasion when the Oath of Allegiance had to be taken, it was found that the Clerk of the Council had left the Bible behind; the ceremony had been delayed by an air raid, and he had forgotten to bring it. Dobbie immediately produced his own pocket Bible, which he always carried with him.

After raids it was always Dobbie's aim to visit the badly hit areas where the casualties were the highest. His interest in the people and his presence inspired them. So too did his courage – perhaps the most infectious of all fine attributes. On such visits he never failed to urge them to keep their faith in God.

Dobbie became their hero. When his car arrived, men would rush forward to open the door for him. They would shake his hand and pat him on the back. He would stay to talk to the people, and always had words of encouragement for them.

On one occasion he found them despondent as they looked at their ruined homes. Dobbie promised them that their houses would be rebuilt as soon as the war was won. At this an old man piped up, 'We will beat the Hun.'

Dobbie replied, 'I see you still retain your spirit!'

He answered, 'Yes sir, I was at Gallipoli. There, at times, we got shot at by our own ships but here we're giving the German aircraft hell!'

Dobbie told him to keep that spirit up – 'Then we can't help but win!' It was a spirit that was certainly needed.

In December 1941, the Germans set out to obliterate the harbour and airfields and destroy all resistance with 600 of the most modern front-line aircraft. In five weeks they destroyed 15,500 buildings, killing or wounding over 3,500 people. In one day they made fourteen raids, and in one raid there were 300 bombers. They dropped over 6,000,000 kg. of bombs, nearly as many as had been dropped in the Battle of Britain! All on a tiny area of only 122 square miles, with a population reckoned in 1962 to be 329,285, compared to England with its 50,875 square miles and a population of 46,000,000. During the whole siege of Malta, the Germans lost at least 1,252 planes and probably another 1,051. The British lost 547 aircraft in the air and 160 destroyed on the ground.

My own special interest in Malta was tied up with its farming and food situation. Having farmed under similar climatic conditions in North Africa, I was in contact with an official at the Ministry of Agriculture who was responsible for Malta's production and storage of food to prevent starvation. For many months the people had only dried pumpkin and goat's meat to live on. Every bit of soil, however small, was made into useful plots, and pumpkins and potatoes were grown and stored in tunnels made in the limestone rock, where they kept in perfect condition.

In many parts of Morocco we stored grain in the same way. The soil would be six to twelve inches deep. A neck would be made in the limestone wide enough for a man to pass through, then a very large hole, somewhat round or bottle-shaped, was hollowed out, filled with grain and then the neck sealed with a large slab of stone and mortar. In wartime, to hide it from an enemy, it would be covered with soil. The limestone is impervious to any dampness and the grain can be kept as long as one likes. So in Malta, pumpkins, potatoes and indeed all food – the first essential in war – were stored underground. This storage was easy, because Malta is made of limestone rock, reasonably easy to burrow into. The surface hardens on exposure to air.

During the raids the population disappeared underground. Consequently, heavy loss of life was avoided. Most of the houses were demolished, but fires too were small, as buildings were made of this local limestone.

When the air raid warnings were heard, our submarines in the harbour submerged and lay at the bottom of the sea. A German bomber pilot, who had been shot down and collected by boat, was asked why, as the submarines were clearly visible on the seabed, they did not come and drop depth charges on them. He scoffed, 'We are not fools. We know those are dummy submarines submerged! Your real ones are in tunnels hollowed out in the limestone.' His captors did not enlighten him; but how short-sighted we had been, not to have built submarine pens in the limestone!

Dobbie's background and earlier career prepared him in many ways for his greatest task. He was born in India on 12 July 1879 and educated at Charterhouse. His forebears had been soldiers, sailors and administrators, first in America and then in India. At the age of fourteen, William Dobbie committed his life to Christ; in 1897 he entered Woolwich as a cadet.

Early in 1901 he went out to South Africa as a 2nd Lieutenant. Soon after embarking he began to hold meetings and Bible studies, attended by between 150 and 200 men. In South Africa he was kept fully occupied as a sapper. His work was inspected and praised by Lord Kitchener.

In 1902 he came home to be married to Sybil Orde Brown whom he had met in his days as a cadet. After marriage he was posted first to Burma and then to Ireland. In the First World War his Royal Engineer units were used for blowing up buildings – later rebuilding them. He was wounded, mentioned in despatches six times, and awarded the D.S.O. After the war he was also awarded the C.M.G and the French *Croix de Guerre* as well as Belgian orders.

He became G.S.O.2 at the War Office and was soon promoted to G.S.O.1. Later he spent some time in Palestine where he gained a reputation both as a modern military mechanization expert and as a Christian general. In 1932 he was appointed Commandant of the School of Military Engineering at Chatham.

He was soon invited to join committees of inter-denominational associations connected with the Services. Two of these were the Army Scripture Readers' Association and the Soldiers' Christian Association (later Soldiers' and Airmen's). He was also a very active member of the Officers' Christian Union and became its chairman.

He soon realized the possibility of the outbreak of another European war. His efforts to mechanize his forces were hampered by the refusal of the government to spend any money on re-armament, which meant that we were unprepared for the Second World War. Britain paid dearly for this unreadiness.

He was also unable to finish his mechanization programme; in 1935 he was sent as General Commander to Malaya. However, at the end of August 1939 he was recalled, and in April 1940 became Governor and Commander in Chief, Malta.

The story of the defence of Malta, and the incredible courage and endurance displayed by everybody, is a proud one. It aroused the admiration of the free world, and more than justified the award to Malta of the George Cross. Never before had such an award, for collective devotion and heroism, been made. There can be no doubt that it was in the divine providence that Dobbie was sent to Malta.

By May 1942, Dobbie was exhausted by the continual strain. He was replaced by Lord Gort. When he landed in England, a wonderful welcome was given to him and he was honoured by the media for his faith in God and his fortitude. He went to

London the next day and had a long conference with the Prime Minister; he was also received by the King who gave him the official accolade for his Knighthood.

He took quite a time to recover from the colossal strain of two years spent in the defence of Malta. While he was in a convalescent home his wife asked him what, if he could choose, he would really like to do above everything else. He replied, 'I should really like to go around the country, telling as many people as I possibly can, about God.' This was a magnificent aim for a great general, K.C.B. and G.C.M.G, a Bailiff Grand Cross of St. John, and a national hero. It was also one which, by the grace of God, he was able to achieve.

The extent of his own faith and reliance upon God was seen most clearly when he was preparing to withstand the sea- and air-borne invasion of Malta. He wrote to Alan Brooke, the CIGS, of his conviction that they had to depend totally upon God since they were so hopelessly outnumbered. He referred to the experience of the prophet Elisha in the Old Testament, who was told by his servant that they were totally surrounded by their enemies, and was asked what they should do. Elisha directed his servant to look to God and not to be afraid: 'We have more on our side than they have on theirs.'

It was with this God that William Dobbie kept in constant contact through his reading of the Bible. That was why he was able to write of his experiences in Malta:

> The faith which many in Malta placed in God was the underlying reason for the fine spirit and courage shown by the people and the garrison, since many were receiving constant reminders that it is no vain thing to put one's trust in God!

7

Air Chief Marshal Sir Wilfrid Freeman Bt. G.C.B., D.S.O., M.C.

Sir Wilfrid Freeman was a man who brought to his work both a steadfast faith in God and a readiness to take calculated risks. We owe an immeasurable debt to his intelligence and judgment. We can never be too thankful for his foresight and leadership, before and during the war, in the research, development and production of aircraft. Lord Hives, of Rolls Royce, said: 'It was the expansion which was carried out under Wilfrid Freeman's direction in 1937–1939 which enabled the Battle of Britain to be won. Without that foresight and imagination, no efforts in 1940 would have yielded any results.'

His interest in aviation dated back to the First World War. He was a Squadron Commander in the Middle East in 1915, and was awarded the D.S.O. and Bar. Later in France with No. 2 Squadron he gained the M.C. after being shot down behind the enemy lines and swimming across the Seine to rejoin his squadron.

The birth of the superb Lancaster bomber in 1938 was the result of Freeman's insistence. The Manchester had proved unsatisfactory. In 1938, Sir Wilfrid Freeman, in his capacity as Air Member for Development and Production, was visiting the business premises of Avro, today known as 'British Aerospace'. In the office of Sir Roy Dobson (Avro's chief designer) he saw a model aeroplane. It had two extra engines and other modifications. Freeman was immediately impressed and authorized Dobson to develop the idea. Through his recognition of the potential of this aircraft our greatest bomber was born – the only plane suitable for use in the famous 'Dam Buster' raids.

I myself had a very brief association with Avro during the war. I went there for a few weeks before starting with MI6/CT6. I spent some time on a training aeroplane made of a new type of laminated wood (I was intrigued to discover that the glue which held it together was made of white of egg!).

The birth of our fastest all-round plane, the Mosquito, was also the result of the genius of Wilfrid Freeman. This was at first dubbed by both his equals and superiors at the Air Ministry 'Freeman's Folly'. But he championed its production against endless opposition, and it proved to be one of the most successful aircraft of World War II. It was largely constructed of balsa wood glued to plywood.

Freeman saw the Mosquito's possibilities from the beginning. Sir Geoffrey de Havilland went ahead privately with its development, and Freeman fought against indifference and stubborn ignorance at the Ministries. After a year he managed to get an order placed for fifty Mosquitoes, but every obstacle was put in the way of obtaining supplies of engines and components. His persistence finally won through, and the Mosquito became the greatest unarmed aircraft used for precision bombing in the war. As its name implies, it had a small, light frame. It also proved to be the most versatile plane used in the war. In the end it was in demand by all commands for all purposes, and stories of its thrilling exploits would easily fill a long book.

Although it was designed as an unarmed bomber,

relying upon speed for safety, it was at first relegated to photo-reconnaisance. Here it was soon realized that no German plane could get near it. Freeman then persuaded Geoffrey de Havilland to demonstrate its incredible bombing potentialities to Air Marshal Sir Arthur Harris. Harris was unwilling to try it out, since he wanted no interference with his heavy 'carpet bombing' of German cities which was causing such heavy loss of life both to his own air-crews and to German civilians. However, Air Commodore Harrison of Bomber Command quickly realized the Mosquito's value and finally convinced Harris of its capabilities. By 1943 it had been developed to carry a load of bombs equal to that of any other bomber, but at 170 mph faster, and also higher.

During the war pilots painted on the nose of their Mosquitos the names of their wives, sweethearts or animals. In the summer of 1944 a Mosquito landed bearing the name 'Folly' on its nose. The other crews wondered why such a name had been given to it. Out stepped Flying Officer Keith Freeman, the twenty-one year old pilot son of Air Marshal Freeman. He had been a schoolboy at Rugby when his father ordered the first fifty Mosquitos, then dubbed 'Freeman's Folly'. The 'Wooden Folly' had now become the 'Wooden Wonder'. It was aptly named! It could sting fatally in the most unexpected places. It was a sturdy plane with amazing endurance. It could bring home its pilot on one engine, survive flying through cables, and even with elevator controls severed, could struggle home to make an adroit belly landing. No wonder pilots called them 'Mossies' – these pugnacious yet friendly little brutes!

It was thanks to Sir Wilfrid Freeman that British aircraft production was stepped up from 2,827 in 1938 to 7,940 in 1939. Between 1940 and 1941 he increased our fighter production to double that of Germany. When the immense German technical ability is taken into account, and also the earlier start which they made on fighter production, this achievement makes one realize the greatness of Freeman's ability. We think of the Battle of Britain as the turning point of the Second World War; but although in one sense it was certainly won by our magnificent pilots, in another sense it had been won beforehand by the dedicated preparation by Freeman and his staff. He had brought together the needs of the RAF for the highest-quality equipment and the maximum capabilities of industry.

In 1942 aircraft production was in danger of falling again. The new Minister of Aircraft Production, Oliver Lyttleton, sent for Freeman, knowing that no one else enjoyed the same degree of confidence of both the RAF and the Ministry. So, in October 1942, Freeman became the Chief Executive, Ministry of Aircraft Production. Both his and Lyttleton's departments rang me frequently to find out if some of my firms could help to supply specialized items.

Freeman himself was able to recognize the skills and abilities of other men in the production of aircraft. In 1939 he had realized the potentials of F. Rodwell Banks and sent him to the Aircraft and Armament Experimental Establishment at Boscombe Down. His talents very soon came to the attention of Lord Beaverbrook, the then Minister of Aircraft Production, who summoned Banks to his home one Saturday morning. By the following Monday morning Banks had formed a new Directorate of Production and Development of Engine Accessories. It became one of my own ports of call – as a Ministry of Supply official – for certain secret accessories.

Early in 1943, Freeman picked out Banks again for

another vital and urgent job – that of counteracting the 'hit and run' raiders which were attacking the South Coast towns. Banks was made responsible for stepping up immediate production of the Sabre. In 1944 he was again sent for to be appointed as Director of Engine Research and Development. Later Rod Banks became an Air Commodore and was awarded the C.B. and O.B.E. and was made a Commander of the Legion of Honour (France) and Commander of the Legion of Merit (U.S.A.). But his abilities would never have come to light had it not been for Freeman.

The Americans, too, owe a debt to Sir Wilfrid Freeman. When the U.S. Air Force penetrated deep into Germany in daylight bombing they suffered very heavy losses. At Schweinfurt on 14 October 1943, out of 291 bombers sent, 198 were destroyed or damaged. To counteract these colossal losses, the Mustang fighter with an Allison engine was produced in the course of six months in America. But it did not prove very effective. Then Freeman and Banks stepped in with the advice to change the engine to a Packard Rolls Royce Merlin. The performance of this engine was phenomenal, and American competence in production ensured that the Merlin/ Mustang concept was turned out in record time. It became a superior fighter with long-range fuel tanks and was used to escort the U.S. Eighth B17s to Berlin.

Sir Wilfrid Freeman's contributions to the war went beyond the production of aircraft, however. Marshal of the RAF, Lord Portal of Hungerford, K.G., G.C.B., O.M., D.S.O., M.C., wrote: 'Freeman virtually took charge of the internal policy governing the enormous war-time expansion of the R.A.F.' Portal admired both Freeman's intelligence and his loyalty and honesty. In his work with the RAF, Freeman had no time for men in high places who were inefficient or too old for their job. When the Secretary of State objected to an appointment put forward by Freeman and Portal the former wrote bluntly, 'Then let's have a new Secretary of State.' When he found that older men were blocking the promotion of their juniors, Freeman wrote to Portal about three of these senior officers:

> They are long past their best and are now incapable of prompt and vigorous action. The first is at the moment on leave . . . and the work proceeds at three times the speed. The second has forgotten the meaning of the word 'decision'. The third is hopelessly senile.

On one occasion Freeman's abilities were called upon to help the situation in North Africa. General O'Connor had made a magnificent advance of 500 miles with two divisions. He had destroyed ten Italian divisions, capturing 130,000 prisoners, 400 tanks and 850 guns at a cost of fewer than 2,000 casualties among his own men. Unfortunately, he was not allowed to push on to Tripoli which would have deprived the enemy of their last base in Africa. As a result the Germans were able to land modern panzer forces in Tripoli which drove our own troops back over the Egyptian border.

During the next few months Churchill made rapid changes in command. He sent Air Chief Marshal Freeman to Cairo with a message to Auchinleck:

> You will find Freeman an officer of altogether larger calibre than the present Commander of the Air Force in Egypt, and if you feel that he would be a greater help to you and that you would have more confidence in the Air Command if he assumed it, you should not hesitate to tell me so . . . .

This was the kind of opinion which Freeman drew from those who worked with him in the war. He would have been the first to admit that his own help came from God. For Freeman was a devout, loyal and generous churchman. A. L. Kennedy in his *Life of Salisbury* states that 'Only trust in God could make a man both lowly and authoritative.' Such a man was Sir Wilfrid Freeman. He did not seek fame, nor to be in the limelight, but it was his work which provided the tools which made such a massive contribution to the Allied victory.

To my mind Freeman was the ablest man of the Second World War. To his intelligence, initiative and persistence we owe a debt that is beyond measure.

Atlantic Charter Banquet
American and British Chiefs of Staff.

8

General Dwight David Eisenhower
G.C.B., O.M.

Many thousands of American troops came to Exmoor, near to where I now live, for pre-D-Day manoeuvres. The Larkbarrow and Tom's Hill area (recently bought by the Department for the Environment) was cleared of its few inhabitants and became the principal training area, while the two farmhouses and other buildings met their inevitable fate. Today the ruins are still to be seen, some distance from the nearest road, bringing back memories of the preparations for the invasion of Europe.

One day, Arthur Saunders, the station master at Dulverton, was informed that a special train would be arriving, but was not told who would be on it. As it approached, he saw it had two sleepers, a dining car, a special saloon car and a cinema car. To his surprise General Eisenhower stepped out, walked over to him, and shook hands, saying, 'I would like to stay for a few days here.' Saunders made a snap decision to keep the General's train where it was and divert other traffic onto a loop line. Looking into the cars he saw there were no flowers, so his wife picked lilies-of-the-valley from their garden and the American staff captain put the vases on the tables. Later on, Eisenhower thanked Mrs. Saunders personally.

When his troop inspections were over, he said to Arthur Saunders, 'I am enjoying myself and would like to stay a bit longer, if you can keep my train where it is.' He hired a horse and enjoyed rides to Winsford and Withypool, two interesting Exmoor villages. When he was leaving he said to the station master, 'I have enjoyed Exmoor enormously. Now I must get back to work.' A month later he launched the greatest armada the world has ever seen – over 5,000 ships.

In 1950, when Eisenhower had become President of the United States, an article in a West of England newspaper recalled his visit to Exmoor. Henry Kingbur, who formerly lived in the area but by then was living in California, saw the article and sent it to the President. Eisenhower replied with a personal note. 'Thank you for mailing me the article', he wrote. 'It brought back memories. I very much enjoyed my few days on Exmoor and I wish they had been more.'

Eisenhower planned his campaign from Abbotsfield, a large thirty-roomed country house near Tavistock, so we of the West Country have a special interest in this fine man.

My own personal interest in him lies in the fact that he made his 'debut' in North Africa – a land where I had farms and had managed the farmlands for the Moroccan royal family. He was keen on the work of our SOE. 'Give me one SOE agent' he said, 'He is worth fifteen divisions.' Eisenhower credited SOE and its activities with shortening the war by at least nine months.

Eisenhower's position in North Africa was very difficult. He got caught up in political problems instead of concentrating solely on military strategy and striking before the Germans were able to build up their forces in Tunisia. This delayed what should have been the rapid conquest of North Africa, and caused considerable loss of life. It was the first time he had commanded an army in action, and his generals and men had no modern battle experience.

But he worked endlessly to get his troops into fighting shape in North Africa. At the beginning of 1943 he wrote that they were inadequately trained. He stressed that it was necessary for all, and especially the junior officers, to be made aware that in such a serious situation thoroughness in every detail was necessary. The mistakes made in manoeuvres at home were being repeated on the battlefield, but this time at the cost of human life. At Kasserine, in North Africa, the same deficiencies were evident and the American campaign was in jeopardy. When the fighting was going especially badly in Algeria, Eisenhower went up to the front to see things for himself and to encourage his men. A German breakthrough was expected at any moment. The commander urged Eisenhower to return by air. He refused, saying that every available aircraft was needed for fighting and not for ferrying generals about.

His position continued to be extremely difficult as he was continually dragged into the political infighting. This was particularly true during 'Operation Torch'. One night as he was returning to his billet he burst out to his driver, whom he often used as a safety-valve, 'I'm a military man, not a politician.' He spent the rest of the drive holding forth vehemently on how the military should not get involved with politics, concluding with, 'It's as important as the separation of church and state.'

Another problem he faced was that of convincing those who worked for him that they were involved in a serious war. He found too much of a 'country club' atmosphere at the American HQ in London, with prolonged lunches, cocktail parties and long week-ends. He swept away all this, starting from the very top. Many Americans were sent back to the states. He also dealt uncompromisingly with anyone who caused disharmony. On one occasion he overheard an American officer boasting that he and his men would show the British what fighting men really were. His reaction was immediate and loud: 'I'll make that sonofabitch swim back to the States!' Much of Eisenhower's time was devoted to forging a united command.

In his contacts with the army he introduced full military discipline; although he could be charming and kind, he was also capable of being tough both with himself and others. Nobody was left in any doubt that he was Supreme Commander. At the same time, he was friendly and approachable. When he summoned young officers to his office, generally to congratulate them, they would enter nervously. But they would come out with glowing faces. He always knew how to put them at their ease.

His personal qualities earned him the devotion of all who served under him. He was a man of high integrity and looked for a similar integrity in others, refusing to tolerate any kind of hypocrisy or untruth-fulness. He was free from any love of the spectacular or ostentatious. He had no ambition for personal fame, but strove to maintain a reputation for uprightness.

Eisenhower's greatness did not lie in his military prowess. Montgomery, who did not always agree with his military tactics, wrote of him:

> I could not class Ike as a great soldier in the true sense of the word. He might have been one if he had ever had the experience of exercising direct command. He had never seen a shot fired in war until the Allied Landings

in North Africa . . . . But he was a great Supreme Commander – a military statesman. He brought the Allied cooperation in Europe to the greatest heights it has ever attained.

It was indeed for his effecting of international unity that Eisenhower is justly famed. He kept the peace between the warring generals and co-ordinated the allied armies into a working unit. He was able to retain the confidence of politicians and had the necessary patience and tact for dealing with them. For example, there was much bitter controversy associated with the planning and execution of 'Operation Overlord'. This he was able to overcome. Under his leadership the Allied Forces came to have a single aim; not to vie with each other, but to unite in the defeat of the German forces. So he was able to lead one of the greatest military operations in history when on D-Day he organized a vast force of aircraft, warships and 4,000 landing craft plus thirty-nine divisions, all in one small area.

What was the secret of such humanity, unselfishness and integrity, in this man who combined warmheartedness and sternness and became one of the best loved men of the War? What was the source of the strength and success of this man who planned such a great invasion force and later took on colossal responsibilities as President of the U.S.A?

The source of Eisenhower's strength is apparent in such incidents as that which happened at a crucial moment in the war, before D-Day, while Eisenhower was staying in Devon. He told his aides to wait, and climbed to the summit of a hill alone. There, aware of his helplessness in such a situation, he turned to God in prayer.

Before his presidency, he studied the life and teaching of Christ in its divine and social realities and determined to take the Bible as 'the rock on which true, free government should rest', believing that 'all men are endowed by their creator with certain inalienable rights'.

Eisenhower's family had come to America from Germany about 1800. They were members of the Russian and German Menonnite Christian Brothers, later known as the Church, or Brethren, of Christ. Theirs was an evangelical form of Christianity. His parents named him after Dwight L. Moody, the great American evangelist who in the nineteenth century preached in both America and England and brought the two countries together in a new spiritual awakening.

The Second World War again broke down the barriers which had built up between the two countries. For Eisenhower it brought the valley of the Thames closer to the farms of Abilene where his family had settled. The honour which meant most to him was the Freedom of the City of London. It was bestowed at a moving ceremony in the ancient Guildhall where his speech stirred those present to tears. He stressed that 'humility must always be the portion of any man who receives acclaim earned in the blood of his followers and the sacrifices of his friends.' He spoke of the true union between the people of America and England which depended on the treasures free men possess: freedom of worship, equality before the law, liberty of speech and action as long as the similar rights of others are not trespassed upon. These, he claimed, belong to all men, whether their homes are in the city of London or the village of Abilene.

At the end of the war Eisenhower was given an insight into the depths of sin into which men who did not acknowledge God could sink. When the American troops began to liberate the 'horror' camps Eisenhower went to one of them accompanied by General Patton. 'Come on, George,' he said. 'We're going through here. I'm not going to let anyone ever say again that all these stories were just made up.' About fifty feet inside the camp General Patton, one of the toughest fighters in the war, became physically ill at what he saw and went outside to wait. General Eisenhower and two others continued their ghastly ordeal. To him it was an outstanding example of 'the exceeding sinfulness of sin'.

At a speech in Pittsburgh Eisenhower said:

> The history of free men is never really written by chance but by choice – their choice. I believe that we have a choice, and that our poverty problem, our race problem, the war problem, are problems of the heart, problems of the spirit. That is the basic crisis, and if we can solve the problems of the spirit, all our other problems can be solved. Therefore I believe it is time that we took our eyes off our shortcomings and failures and put them on Christ, who said, 'You must be born again'.

After his death Eisenhower was given a simple burial in the tiny chapel in the quiet town where he had spent his youth. There the pastor gave thanks for his life and that of his parents. We can, indeed, thank God that such a man as Eisenhower was raised up when he was most needed. We can also find in his life and principles our own inspiration to be ready to apply ourselves to any worth-while task that comes to hand.

9

'Colonel Passy' of the Deuxième Bureau

At midnight, Captain André Dewavrin boarded the last ship escaping from Brest after the surrender of France. He was twenty-eight years old, young, fair-haired and charming. A regular soldier, he had been awarded a D.S.O. and M.C. for his great courage and efficiency in the Norwegian campaign.

On landing in England he made his way to General de Gaulle's HQ at St. Stephen's House, Westminster. After an interview of an hour and a half, de Gaulle gave him permission to start a section of the Free-French *Deuxième Bureau* (Secret Intelligence Service) in England.[1]

Like many of us in the Second World War, he had been given a job about which he knew nothing. He had been through Saint-Cyr, the Sandhurst of France, and had also excelled himself in France's élite School of Engineers. In Norway he had proved his ability and adaptability.

He set to work and collected a small staff. One of his first moves was to get himself and them out of

1. The French Deuxième Bureau centralizes and interprets intelligence, and presents it to the High Command. This intelligence comes from various sources such as their espionage section, the SR (Service de Renseignments) and the CE (Counter-Espionage). The Deuxième Bureau also collects information from the Press and other forms of the media, from the Diplomatic Service and from friendly foreign sources. They collate and synthesize all facts to pass on to the High Command. The Deuxième Bureau and its associated Secret Services was set up after France's defeat by Germany in 1871.

uniform and into civilian clothes, a wise move and one which I had insisted upon for myself for my own secret work, when it had been suggested that I should wear the uniform of a major. The next step was to adopt cover names. If the Gestapo found out the identities of these men, their families in France would suffer. So André became 'Colonel Passy', taking his name from the Metro in Paris.

He set up his French Organization at 10 Duke Street behind Selfridges and it soon became one of my ports of call as I supplied their agents with secret equipment of every sort – Gauloise cigarettes, French matches, Menier chocolate and so on – all made up by my English firms as exact replicas of the originals.

I also had French women agents to supply. Madame Rigby, of 5 South Molton Street, provided super French underwear. Other items were also needed. André's staff were able to collect well-worn valises from Frenchmen, as they arrived after fleeing from France. I wanted these for our own SOE agents going to France. The original owners received new British leather cases, and never knew to whom they owed their good fortune!

Dewavrin was soon in contact with 'Uncle Claude' (Deputy Director of MI6 – Sir Claude Dansey). Plans were set in motion to train *Deuxième Bureau* agents for work in France. As the work grew and expanded it was given a new title – BCRA (*Bureau Central de Renseigments et d'Action*), an organization combining intelligence gathering and sabotage. They relied on the SOE to train their agents and for transport of fire-arms and other supplies from my department.

Dewavrin was then asked to produce a network of agents to obtain full information about Hitler's Atlantic Wall which was being built against an invasion of allied forces, especially along the coast-line of Normandy, from Cherbourg to Le Havre. Immediately there flashed into Dewavrin's mind the man for the job; a man who already had excellent experience and who had been extremely successful. There could be no one more suitable to start a new network than Renault.

Some months later the tables in Dewavrin's office were covered with flimsy maps and reports sent in by Renault's agents. He was flabbergasted at what they revealed. He lifted his secret scrambler telephone and called the Deputy Director of MI6. The maps and information were taken to a bomb-proof base-ment in Storey's Gate, quite near my office. In fifteen days it was all pieced together, and there was the plan of Hitler's so-called impregnable Atlantic Wall, with its roads, gun emplacements, airfields and oil dumps. It was discovered that the siting of the bunkers and block houses adhered to the old Siegfried Line specifications, which simplified the situation. The whole area was then checked by aerial photography and the material from France was confirmed as accurate and of the highest value.

On D-Day the Allies knew, for instance, the exact position and strength of a block house, thanks to the work of these agents. A workman would walk into a café and sit down at a table. In the spare seat another man would sit down, who would in fact be an agent. After a time, the agent would remark that the concrete walls of the big block house looked pretty thick – about two feet, perhaps. The workman, his pride offended, would then declare that they were double that thickness. When the workman got up to return to work, the agent, who by now had established a friendly relationship with him, also rose, discussing some matter or other until they reached the barrier.

The agent then got into conversation with the sentry, and, out of the corner of his eye, noted how many steps the workman took from the barrier to the block house. (Further details of the gathering of information can be found in *The Secret War of Charles Fraser-Smith*.)

Checking became precise and swift. When Air Reconnaisance reported to Dewavrin that a small and sinister looking concrete structure had gone up rapidly between two block houses in this area they pressed for details. Within a week the answer came back – a shower bath!

Early in 1943 the SOE decided that André should go to France to check up the whole situation and to re-organize the Free-French Resistance. In certain important respects they were jeopardizing the work we were doing. The French National Council of Resistance had tried to prove to us that their secret army was 100,000 strong and needed immediately eighty arms supply dropping operations. We had warned them that it was dangerous for their Resistance to be under a unified command, that it was too centralized, and that it had been mobilized much too far in advance of an invasion date, so we had to refuse to endanger our aircraft on such an operation. Our calculated forecast had proved sadly correct. General Delestraint (code name Vidal) and his deputy had been captured, and the organization dispersed. They had refused to follow our system of small groups or cells, so André Dewavrin needed to go to impress on his compatriots the absolute necessity of adopting our system in order to prepare for invasion day.

At first MI6 refused permission for André to go, on the grounds that he knew too much. If the Gestapo captured him, he could not be sure how he would react or what he might say under extreme torture. So Dewavrin went to see de Gaulle. He wore a special signet ring I had supplied, which had secreted inside it a cyanide pill – for use in case of capture by the Gestapo – and this he produced. After de Gaulle had scrutinized this determined young man he picked up the telephone and rang Churchill. The ban was lifted. A few days later Dewavrin went to our depot at Tempsford and was fitted out with the necessary equipment from my supplies. On 27 February he parachuted from a Halifax into a cornfield near Lyons-la-Forêt, some twenty miles from Rouen.

He had sent ahead of him two top Resistance men to start preparing the way, Pierre Brosselette, who had been a journalist before the war, and Yeo-Thomas, who was a director of Molyneux in Paris and who escaped to England when France surrendered. They had vital discussions with Resistance leaders and persuaded them to separate intelligence work from sabotage, so that neither 'sabotaged' the other. As Hitler had over 300,000 workmen engaged on strengthening the Atlantic Wall, Resistance groups were strengthened to help to send information about all improvements and alterations.

André was also able to organize key plans for D-Day. There was the 'Green Plan', to sabotage railway engines and cut railway lines. Our bombing could deal with important rail junctions. There was the 'Red Plan', for cutting all telephone wires and sabotaging key points. 'Operation Turtle' was for strategic stalling of German road transport and the destruction of certain bridges.

The final question Dewavrin was asked before returning to London was when and where the Allied landing would take place. We had not given him this information. If he had been able to tell them, and they had realized that they had some twelve months to prepare, it would have discouraged them. He certainly could not give them the slightest idea of where. So he shrugged his shoulders and said positively, 'I have no idea. You have got to have faith.'

On one matter Dewavrin is exceptionally humble. If you pay tribute to his vision and courage in bringing about a great victory for the intelligence service he replies, 'No, no, it is the others you have to write about, because they had faith. Very much like the Bible – you know – what Paul said in the book of Hebrews. He talks about men of faith like Noah, Abraham and others, and he called faith "the substance of things hoped for, the evidence of things not seen".'

Men like Dewavrin continued day after day against great odds and with little or no encouragement, not knowing if their hard and dangerous work was recognized or being used because of the necessity for complete secrecy. All their work had to be done in faith.

For André Dewavrin, faith was a key to his whole view of life. Like the majority of his countrymen, he was, I understand, a Roman Catholic. For Dewavrin and many like him, the outbreak of war was the beginning of a time of when the quiet observance of religion over a lifetime was revealed to have laid the foundations of a faith that proved itself in time of trial. In this sense, the War produced countless numbers of men (and women) of faith who will never be celebrated in books such as this, yet – like all those included here – found that their faith was a deep resource when circumstances turned dangerous and perplexing.

10

'Colonel Rémy'

Another French agent with Christian convictions was Colonel Gilbert Renault-Roulier. After his death he was described in the *Daily Telegraph* as 'France's foremost wartime intelligence chief'. A truer description would have been 'foremost secret intelligence agent'. By profession he was a film producer and in 1940 he was in Spain directing a historical film on the life of Christopher Columbus. After the fall of France he came to England on a Norwegian cargo boat, landing at Falmouth. He presented himself to André Dewavrin. The first thing that impressed André was Renault's volubility. If necessary, he would certainly be able to talk his way out of any situation! What also interested André was that Renault had up-to-date Spanish and French visas. This meant he could freely enter Spain and France without all the difficulties and dangers of having to be smuggled in.

He received training and left for France in a Sunderland flying boat in August 1940, travelling via Portugal and Spain. The principal pseudonym he operated under was 'Colonel Rémy'. Soon, coded flimsies of vital importance started to arrive in Dewavrin's office, causing great excitement. There were reports of the movements of the German battle-ships *Scharnhorst* and *Gneisenau,* and of various other shipping in Bordeaux, Brest, Lorient, Quiberon and other ports, with maps showing airfields and oil refineries.

His greatest maritime coup was his discovery that the German battleship *Bismarck,* after devastating raids on our shipping in the Atlantic, was returning to a French port for refitting. He radioed London, and British warships met the German raider and sank her.

In February 1942 Renault received an urgent message to return to England. A Lysander picked him up near Rouen and brought him to Tangmere, Sussex. The Intelligence officer who met him was amazed to see that he had three full sacks with him. He asked where they should be deposited. Renault casually said, 'They are dispatches from my network.'

Dewavrin then instructed Renault to set up networks for sending back information about the Atlantic Wall, the strip of land, twelve miles in depth, along the coast eastwards from Cherbourg, which Hitler was fortifying in order to repulse an allied invasion. A whole book could be written about the methods Renault used to carry out this programme and about the remarkable and valuable information he sent back concerning the fortifications of this Atlantic Wall. As the Germans finally got on his trail Renault, his wife and family were brought out by sea. It was feared they would be seized and used as hostages by the Germans.

The ship used was a French fishing vessel which had brought over refugees after Dunkirk. Her hull and superstructure were painted in Breton colours as the operation was to take place off the coast of Brittany. Arrangements were made for a rendezvous at a certain point off the Iles de Glenans. The first attempt was called off just as the boat was about to sail. On the second attempt, when the party arrived, they saw a boat approaching from the islands. It did not respond to the pre-arranged signal and passed harmlessly by. The RAF then suddenly appeared and attacked the ports and, unfortunately for Renault, they dropped mines which closed all ports and no vessels were allowed out.

At the third attempt, while the ship was waiting at the rendezvous, three German minesweeping trawlers appeared. The crew lowered their trawl and began fishing! The Germans passed by within 500 yards but took no notice beyond scrutinizing them through binoculars. No sooner had they passed than a small boat was seen approaching from behind one of the islands, but only three men could be seen in it. However, it responded to the recognition signal and came alongside. From hiding emerged Madame Renault, three children and Renault himself with a very small baby under one arm and a full briefcase under the other. There were also several suitcases. It was extraordinary that so much had been concealed in such a small boat. Considering that there was a Heinkel flying overhead, a German armed trawler passing by, later followed by three German destroyers, all of whom miraculously ignored the innocent-seeming 'French fishing vessel', it is amazing that they got away from the fishing-zone limit that night and arrived safely in England without incident.

A week had not gone by before Renault decided that he should go back to France. But he realized that he would have to change his appearance. He did not tell his wife of his intention but she soon spotted that he was growing a moustache and asked him if he was going back to France. When he replied that he was, she demanded to know why he had brought her to England, for now she would not be able to help him and provide periods of relaxation for him in his dangerous work. When, however, she realized that his network of agents needed him she said no more.

Before he returned to France he was made to look twenty years older. Theatrical tricks enabled him to acquire a stoop and a larger girth, and he was given shoes that added to his height. He was also sent to a dentist. But when he saw the dentist approaching with a pair of forceps to remove his teeth he jumped out of the chair. That was taking it too far!

Not only did his disguise deceive his best friends in France; but German soldiers, seeing his advanced age, would even offer him their seats in railway carriages. There was always a great danger that if people recognized an agent, they would not be able to resist mentioning it to someone else. Some people always wanted to prove they knew what was going on, especially anything of a secret nature, and that information could filter through to the Gestapo.

Renault made several journeys between England and France, under very difficult conditions. Again and again he would say good-bye to his wife and family, and arrive at Falmouth, only to find that weather conditions had deteriorated, or else messages would arrive that the reception party off the coast of France could not meet him. He would return to his home and await new arrangements. These partings were heart-breaking for his wife. Fear continually gripped their hearts and immense courage was needed to face these situations.

Often at the last moment, when so much had happened to delay a journey, Renault himself felt that he could not go ahead. He bravely admitted that had he not been too ashamed to do so, he would have given anything and done anything, to avoid going. He summed it up: 'Courage – or what by general agreement is called courage – is very often nothing else than the desire to correspond with the idea that other people have of you. I valued the opinion of my friends.'

When going to France, he often went to Penzance by train and an RAF launch would take him to the Scilly Islands. He would then write his wife a letter full of assumed confidence, as much to encourage himself as to reassure her. At St. Mary's the Breton fishing trawler would be waiting for him. Near the French coast he would be transferred to a small fishing boat which had a concealed compartment, or a false bottom put into the keel.

Another feat Renault helped to make possible was the famous raid on the German radar station at Bruneval, where a system was operating which helped the Luftwaffe to track our aircraft and enabled German night fighters to take a heavy toll of our bombers. Renault and his team reconnoitred this Wurzburg installation, ascertaining full details of its defence and where a raiding party could be evacuated by sea after action. It was on top of a 400 foot cliff but fortunately a slope nearby led down to a small beach which in the past had been known as the *Descente des Anglais*. It was certainly used effectively in this raid. Three 'sticks' of Paras were dropped, who dealt with the German guards, whilst technicians dismantled the vital parts of the radar, and the Navy evacuated the raiders and their booty.

News of this first effective landing in France since its fall spread like wild-fire, giving the people hope for the future and putting fresh heart into those who were joining the Resistance and gathering information for our agents.

At the beginning of 1944 we called upon Renault to form a special group of Frenchmen to obtain certain vital information essential for D-Day and after. He went to Algeria and selected non-military French recruits, whittling them down to eighty-seven. He brought them to England for secret and rapid intensive training. This group was kept apart from all other secret sections. In fact, even de Gaulle knew nothing about it. We had no confidence in de Gaulle. Instead of concentrating on defeating Hitler, he was continually and arrogantly asserting his own authority, and he refused to cooperate with our SOE in France, which often weakened our efforts. His unreliability and wilfulness were proverbial. At one time, in 1942, he asked Molotov, the Soviet Foreign Minister, who was on a visit to London, whether he would be prepared to admit him and his Free French forces to Soviet territory as he wished to sever relations with America and Britain. So every precaution was taken to keep this top-secret group, and the place and date of D-Day, from de Gaulle.

Renault played a magnificent part in this. When de Gaulle realized that the invasion of France must be near he sent one of his high ranking officers, who was friendly with Renault and had been a great help to him in his intelligence work, to ask where and when the landing would be made. This officer walked to the map on the wall in Renault's office and, pointing to the Normandy coast, asked if he knew whether or not that was the area. But Renault's orders from Eisenhower were absolute, though it hurt him not to be able to tell his great friend anything at all, and the officer was equally distressed.

At about the same time a leading American arrived at Renault's HQ whilst he was in conference. The officer in charge at the door demanded, 'Are you bigoted?' Being a liberal attorney, the American was flustered and offended and replied, 'Of course not'. He went off in a temper when he was asked to leave immediately. Later he learnt that BIGOT was the code-word for those few who alone knew when and where the Allied forces would land.

This special top-secret group, organized and controlled by Renault alone, was equipped with my secret gadgets, weapons and transmitter sets. Each one had to be provided with authentic clothing and effects, down to Gibbs dentifrice tins and every conceivable type of false document and ration card.

No one else in the British Secret Service or in those of America or France knew who these men were. Nor did the enemy have time to discover their identity as they were landed only shortly before D-Day. They were virtually unknown to each other, having trained in small groups. Each individual was dropped in a certain area of Normandy and forbidden to leave that area, thus avoiding any infiltration by the enemy or betrayal of the others if one was caught and tortured. Not only did each man transmit back vital intelligence, but when it was put together, it confirmed what our SOE and the French Secret Service were sending back, and proved that no group had been infiltrated by the enemy.

These top secret precautions had to be taken as General de Gaulle and his close followers had become politically power-hungry and untrustworthy. We found that de Gaullists in Algeria were ousting and imprisoning political opponents, even those who had bravely assisted our landings. The followers of de Gaulle, seeing victory ahead, had now started the same tactics in France, and resistance leaders and agents who were not pro-Gaullist were even being betrayed to the Gestapo!

Renault became one of the cleverest and most successful French agents of the Second World War but at the same time he loathed all the intrigue, deception and lies. He was a man of sterling character, who was prepared to modify some of his Christian principles because he was convinced of the righteousness of the Allied cause. In ordinary life he was completely straightforward, but he considered that deceiving the Germans was part of a righteous crusade. His habit of self-effacement and his modesty disguised the fact that he was a shrewd man of action with great ability and powers of leadership. He was unselfish to the point of saintliness and he was sustained by his faith in God.

My own special contribution to Renault's work was to keep the cafés in France supplied with dominoes. Renault would contact his agents in a café over a game of dominoes. When he took on a new agent he would ask if he played dominoes. If he didn't he was instructed to become fully acquainted with the game. It was a good cover for talking secretly and also a means of secreting and passing coded messages. I supplied hundreds of sets of dominoes, not only for POW camps, but also to agents in France through the *Deuxiéme Bureau*. A domino made a useful hiding place for small compasses and maps, secret messages and other items.

After D-Day Renault remained in France and acted as liaison officer between our advancing forces and the Resistance behind the enemy lines. After the war he retired with his family to Portugal. He was one of France's most highly decorated wartime heroes and became a prolific historian of the French Resistance. One of his works, in two large volumes, is called *Le Livre du Courage et de la Peur*. He presented copies of these volumes to Captain Ridley, my opposite number in MI6, whose son, Vice-Admiral W. T. C. Ridley, kindly loaned them to me. Renault's inscription on the flyleaf is reproduced below.

At the fortieth anniversary of the D-Day landings Renault was given a prominent position in the ceremony. A few weeks later, in August 1984, at the age of seventy-nine he died, having 'fought the good fight and finished the course'.

Rémy's reseau, or network, was called *La Confrèrerie de Notre Dame* (The Brotherhood of Our Lady).

To Captain Ridley: a witness to my gratitude for all he did to enable our Lady of Victory to take her place once more in London.

His final message to his *Confrérerie* after disbandment was:

> A ceux de mon reseau qui ont souffert dans leur chair, fait de courage et de peur, de larmes et de rires, d'angoisses et de torture, de misère et de sang.
>
> (Signed)   Rémy.
>
> Noel 1945

> To those who have suffered in their flesh—members of my network, woven with gallantry and fear, tears and laughter, anguish and torture, misery and blood.
>
> (Signed)   Rémy.
>
> Christmas 1945

11

Lieutenant-General Sir Arthur Smith,
K.C.B., K.B.E., D.S.O., M.C., LL.D.

Arthur Francis Smith was born in Derbyshire in 1890. His father, Colonel Granville Smith, had served with distinction in the Coldstream Guards. At Eton Arthur Smith excelled in athletics, rowed for his school and was a good horseman. He was commissioned from Sandhurst into his father's regiment. He maintained his sporting interest and he also organized Bible studies wherever he went. It is for his founding of so many Bible Study groups that he is, above all, remembered.

In World War I he was mentioned in dispatches five times, awarded the DSO, MC and the *Croix de Guerre*. Three times he was seriously wounded. While recovering in a nursing home he met the Hon. Monica Crossley and they were married in 1918. Though he underwent fourteen operations to repair a shattered leg, the bone that had been splintered never properly grew together again. He overcame the physical limitation by force of will, and his widow, by then the Hon. Lady Monica Smith, recalled: 'He became able to walk *miles* on rough ground without any kind of support . . . . the muscles and the tibia kept him going.'

Although he was as strict a disciplinarian in the home as he was professionally, his family had the deepest love for him and he had the joy of seeing them all become sincere Christians.

Between the wars Arthur Smith's Christian influence at Sandhurst was immense and he was able to help cadets to study and understand the Bible more than any adjutant or commander of that day. A booklet which he compiled, *100 Days,* was a series of One Hundred Bible Studies on selected topics. It was written to help the Sandhurst cadets understand their Bible, but it was much more widely successful – at his death the number of copies printed, in several languages, approached 200,000.

There is no doubt, either, that he had an extremely practical Christian outlook. He had a genuine interest in the welfare of his men and in that of the widows of those who had been killed on active service. He was responsible for the building of married quarters and gave generous support to many charities. Nobody knows how many were helped and spiritually inspired by this man in their daily lives and with their many problems.

In 1938 he was appointed Wavell's Chief of Staff in the Mid-East. Wavell described Arthur Smith as 'a very fine character indeed, a charming personality and an excellent staff officer, very conscientious and accurate, was the very soul of honour and uprightness, organised staff well, ran an extremely happy show, and had a delightful sense of humour.'

When Lt. Col. Miles Reid arrived in Cairo on his way to Greece he presented his credentials to General Sir Arthur Smith. Miles Reid states how Arthur Smith's help proved invaluable to him as he prepared a special liaison unit for the Greek campaign. Reid found him little changed from what he had been in the First World War. He was greyer, with more lines in his face; but he looked a most impressive general. As soon as they were alone Reid found that the outward insignia of his high rank had made no difference to him. He still retained his infectious Christian straightforwardness and enthusiasm which endeared him to all, while at the same time he still inspired the greatest respect and admiration.

This is illustrated by the following extract from a letter written by Lord Ballantrae (formerly Bernard Ferguson) to Lady Monica Smith on the death of her husband, in 1977.

> General Arthur had always meant a very great deal to me ever since I first met him when I was a G.C. at Sandhurst. I was 19. That was the beginning of an association and friendship which has been precious to me ever since. It became close when I was A.D.C. to Archie Wavell at Aldershot in 1935–7, and closer still in those historic Cairo days of 1941, when General Arthur was an inspiration to us all.
>
> During the Crete evacuation, members of the G.H.Q. staff attending the usual bi-weekly meeting were sitting around the table *steeped* in gloom and despondency. General Arthur came in late (probably for the first time in his life) and said to the assembled company something like this:- 'Gentlemen, the news from Crete is very bad, and don't let's pretend it isn't. But equally, don't let's forget that we are fighting on the side of God, and that we shall win in the end. Now to business.'
>
> It brightened us all up, even those who were short on faith: and from that moment the whole spirit of G.H.Q. took on a new hope.

When the Germans reached the borders of Eygpt, Sir Miles said of Arthur Smith, 'He remained calm and collected as usual, inspiring confidence. He does not minimise facts but states them clearly. He makes no bones that we are in for extremely difficult days. That is the sort of thing one wants at times like these.'

His steadfastness was invaluable in the vicissitudes of the Desert War. The situation was critical. If the Germans had broken into Cairo, they would have swept into Arabia and obtained the oil they so badly needed. In this situation many Egyptians were not only anti-British, they were pro-German and they did not want to be on the losing side. King Farouk was insisting that it was his duty to keep his people out of the war. Fortunately orders were given to ring the King's palace with tanks and the ambassador marched in and told the monarch to act or to abdicate. The decision came not a moment too soon. German gunfire could be heard. Churchill was flown to the area, General Auchinleck was replaced by General Alexander, and General Montgomery took command in the desert; General Rommel was kept on the retreat for 1,000 miles.

General Arthur Smith was so highly thought of that Churchill himself offered him command of a corps. He declined this, believing that he did not possess sufficient experience of tanks and aeroplanes and other mechanics of modern warfare.

In 1942/3 he was GOC London, with a quarter of a million under his command and then Alan Brooke, CIGS, appointed him Commander in Chief, Persia and Iraq Command. Here he had the responsibility of maintaining a line through Persia, supplying over 5,000,000 tons of war material to Russia. This was a military backwater for his troops, but it was a job of paramount importance and he made a splendid job of keeping up the morale of his men. He also established good relationships with the local tribesmen.

Alan Brooke wrote in his diary: 'There is no doubt that Arthur Smith is a very fine man, entirely selfless and with only one thought – that of serving his country.'

At the end of 1945 Arthur Smith was moved to India, becoming the Commander of the British Troops in India and Pakistan. These years were filled with great problems and many political difficulties as power was transferred. In these circumstances his courtesy and impartiality proved invaluable.

After his retirement in 1948 Arthur Smith became active in a large number of Christian organizations both at home and abroad. He was involved in the Crusader Union, becoming its President, and also in the Evangelical Alliance. He also became Chairman of Dr. Barnardo's Homes, the Officers' Christian Union, the Soldiers' and Airmen's Scripture Readers' Association and the Africa Inland Mission. He continued to be in demand as a speaker. He had an acute dislike of long-windedness. At a large SASRA gathering a few military and airforce men had given short talks concerning faith in God. The chairman turned to General Sir Arthur Smith and asked if he would like to give a final word. There was a hush of expectancy as he went to the microphone. His opening statement, 'My name is Smith', was greeted by peals of laughter. Then he went on, 'And my testimony and witness is that God saves and God keeps.' With these simple and effective words he returned to his seat. They were typical of the man, 'every inch a soldier and every inch a Christian'.

12

Field Marshal Viscount Alanbrooke,
K.G., G.C.B., O.M. G.C.V.O., D.S.O.

Viscount Alanbrooke (Alan Brooke) was never in the headlines, yet his was the controlling hand on the other great men of the nineteen-forties. He was said to be the only man who was able to apply a necessary, though often very unwelcome, curb on Churchill's ideas and enthusiasms. General Montgomery wrote:

> It is my opinion that Brooke and Churchill together did more to ensure that we won the Second World War than any other men. They were a great pair. And in spite of all that he is and all that he has done, Brooke is the most retiring and modest man I have ever met.

Viscount Alanbrooke came from a northern family of fighting baronets. He went to Woolwich, and served with distinction in the First World War. He was mentioned six times in Despatches, and ended the war as a Lieutenant-Colonel with D.S.O. and Bar and a *Croix-de-Guerre*. From then on his range of experience was unequalled in any of the services.

During the Second World War he proved to be completely unshakeable. In fact, he could withstand shocks and disasters better than the Prime Minister himself. He always considered it of primary importance to hide every trace of his inner feelings. Knowing how quickly fear can spread, he always sought to appear completely confident.

In dealing with others, and especially with Churchill, he showed tremendous patience and self-control. He proved to be a resolute and iron-willed commander, demanding absolute efficiency and speed of thought and action. He was a giant of a man, with a steadfast faith in God, and with the kind of well balanced brain that could lead the Allies to victory against the colossal and evil might of Germany.

Despite the habitual self-effacement of Viscount Alanbrooke glimpses are gradually emerging of his greatness and ability. There is no doubt that he was the ablest British soldier at Dunkirk. He fought a magnificent battle, despite inadequate and outdated equipment, and the Germans sustained heavy losses. In spite of the disarray of the French army, he achieved a great military feat in bringing our forces to the coast for evacuation through the closing jaws of an enemy vastly superior in equipment, and with men who had had battle experience in Poland.

Soon after Dunkirk, Churchill, recognizing his ability, entrusted him with the command of forces to repel invasion and he was appointed Chief of the Imperial General Staff (CIGS), a position he held until the end of the war. He was in daily consultation with the Prime Minister and (fortunately) accompanied him on his wartime journeys and to conferences.

In choosing General Sir Alan Brooke to be CIGS, Churchill had chosen a much stronger man than Dill, his predecessor. Brooke was a tougher man, less inclined to compromise, with greater intelligence; and he was a skilled strategist. It was with strategy and not mere tactics that he concerned himself, and time has proved him to have been the greatest coordinator of every major wartime operation as well as a wise counsellor to those in the highest positions.

His first and never-ending task was the handling of Churchill. He had to confine the P.M's visions to practical realities. He fearlessly withstood Churchill's excesses – ideas which ranged from the most brilliant to the most dangerous conceptions. Fortunately Churchill recognized Brooke's ability to separate the wheat from the chaff. He was consistently level-headed and uncompromising in regard to military matters. No arguments, entreaties, or even abuse from Churchill could move him. He remained firm in his resolve that military decisions must be taken by professional soldiers, and that his political boss must not be allowed to interfere. He wrote in his diary, 'Difficult times with the P.M. I see clearly ahead of me. I pray God to give me guidance as to how to handle the situation which will confront me.' Although the relationship was, at times, very tempestuous, a wonderful, unbroken understanding and partnership was maintained throughout the war.

Once, when Churchill was infuriated because he could not overcome Brooke's continued opposition to a favourite project, he said to General Ismay, a principal adviser in the War Cabinet, that Brooke must hate him and would have to go. Ismay reported this to Brooke who replied, 'I don't hate him – I love him – but when the day comes that I tell him he is right when I believe him to be wrong, it will be time for him to get rid of me.' In Brooke's diaries he openly expressed his views on these matters and when he read them Churchill never forgave Brooke. That is possibly why we heard so little of Brooke's greatness and his invaluable work in the overall prosecution of the war.

Brooke was also fearless in his opposition to Air Marshal Harris and his popular programme of the all-out bombing of German cities. When Montgomery pointed out the need for aircraft to co-operate fully with ground forces, Brooke wrote in 1942, 'We are now reaping the full disadvantage of an all-out independent Air Policy directed at the bombing of Germany. As a result, we are short of all suitable types of aircraft for support of the other two services. It is an uphill battle to fight.' Air Marshal Harris insisted that bombers alone could win the war, and that he might have won the war himself, if it had not been for the handicap imposed by the existence of the other two services!

Events proved otherwise and many military and naval set-backs were the result of this unbalanced insistence on excessive bombing of Germany. Instead of causing loss of production and breaking their resistance, it increased production and strengthened their will to resist. Harris also refused to supply even a few aircraft for the vital work of SOE in the transport of secret agents, and supplying of arms to the Resistance groups in preparation for D–Day. This too was, in my opinion, completely wrong.

Another of Brooke's great achievements was his recognition of the magnificent fighting and leadership qualities of Montgomery. He realized that Montgomery would need a judicious combination of restraint and encouragement. Montgomery also realized this. Even before Dunkirk he wrote: 'My Corps Commander was General Brooke. We had been together at the Staff College. All his orders were very clear. He handled me very well. He saved me from getting into trouble and always backed me when others wanted to down me.'

I particularly like Montgomery's letter to Alan-brooke, written after the end of the war.

There have been moments when I have gone 'off the rails', due to impetuosity, irritation or some such reason. You always pulled me back on the rails . . . it increased your work . . . you never complained. I want to say – first, I am terribly grateful for all you have done for me, second, I could never have achieved anything without your help . . . wise guidance, and your firm handling of a very difficult subordinate. Thank you very much Brookie. You have been a true friend at all times.

When Brooke reprimanded Montgomery for impairing relationships with Eisenhower, he noted in his diary, 'Monty, as usual, was most grateful for having his failings pointed out to him.' If, at times, Monty's staff felt he was determined on some course of his own with which they disagreed, their last resource was to ask, 'Have you consulted the CIGS, sir?' If he had, then they were fully satisfied.

Possibly the most critical time in the lives of Brooke and Montgomery, and of world history, was after the Cairo conference in August 1942. Rommel was preparing a drive through Egypt to obtain the oil fields of the Middle East. We were preparing to evacuate Cairo and Egypt. Churchill, Smuts of South Africa, and Brooke arrived in Cairo to confer. Churchill and Smuts both wanted Alexander to take charge of the battle. But it was Brooke who had the best knowledge of the men under him. He told them that Montgomery was the man to put new life into the Eighth Army and to gain the tactical victory. Alexander could bring about the situation in which the genius and ability of Montgomery could be put to good effect.

Montgomery was summoned to Egypt and immediately after his arrival he toured the front. Brooke wrote in his diary:

I thought I knew my Monty well; but I must confess that I was dumbfounded by the rapidity with which he had grasped the essentials, the clarity of his plans and his unbounded self-confidence – a self-confidence with which he inspired all those with whom he came in contact. I went to bed that night with a wonderful feeling of contentment.

It had not been an easy matter to get Churchill to accept Monty in command of the Eighth Army. As Brooke left Egypt he wrote to Montgomery: 'A short line to tell you how happy I am to feel that the Eighth Army is in your care. Look after yourself, don't work too hard, and may God give you all the help and assistance you may require. God bless you. Yours ever, Brookie.'

In his diary, 18 August 1942, he wrote: 'I pray to God that the new Alexander-Montgomery combination will be a success. I can think of nothing better.' Two months later, at El Alamein, Rommel's army was in full retreat.

One of Brooke's most difficult tasks was the handling of the American generals. General Marshall, head of the American Military Forces, considered that the priority objective was the crossing of the Channel and the defeat of Germany in Europe, and not the campaign in North Africa. General Brooke, who had practical fighting experience, and was able to take a global view of the war, had studied all the statistics and had them at his finger-tips.

It was Brooke's advice that eventually prevailed. The first necessity was to drive the Germans and Italians out of the whole of North Africa and gain control of the Mediterranean. Until this was done there would not be enough shipping to stage any major operation. Such control would also have a profound psychological effect on Italy, France and the Balkans, giving a stimulus to all the Resistance groups and leading to widespread harrassment of the enemy. Brooke was proved right. As the Allies crossed the Mediterranean, the Germans had to pour men into Italy and southern Europe, dissipating their strength and making possible the landing in France and the Russian advance.

In this way the scene was set for the supreme strategy of the final stage of the great drama of D-Day, unobtrusively engineered by a man who was never in the limelight and whose colossal achievements were never fully recognized. It was Brooke who should have led the invasion force, which to begin with was predominantly British, into Europe, but unfortunately Roosevelt overruled matters and Churchill had to acquiesce in the President's selection of General Eisenhower. Brooke was too great a man to express his acute disappointment at the time.

If even today the question were asked as to who, if not the greatest and wisest man in the war, was at least the most balanced, probably only one in a million would give the right answer.

Like many great and celebrated people, Brooke was a person who loved the simple things of life. During the war, on fine evenings, he would slip into Kew Gardens. He enjoyed its peace and found rest in the contact with God through nature.

He was also a great family man. His few weekends at home meant everything to him. In his diaries he refers to his 'beloved companion', and looks forward to the time when he will be able to be continually with her. Even at the height of his military career he wrote to his wife: 'Another day gone, and thank God for it. Every day that passes must at least be one less day of the war. There are times when the madness and fallacy of war almost choke me. I long for a peace that will allow us to spend the remaining years of our life quietly together in a cottage and garden – somewhere where I can bask in the sublime happiness of the sunshine of your company. I thank God for allowing me to know you.'

He spent time with his children, building goat-carts and drawing nonsense sketches of animals. At a surprise home visit one day he found them all singing hymns. It was a wet and depressing day but he wrote, 'It might have been brilliant sunshine for the joy of being with you for a few hours.' It was in order to educate his children that he sold his former house. After the war he did indeed retire to a cottage and there quietly immersed himself in public duties and country pursuits.

This was no hardship for it was in such pursuits that he found much joy. When he was bird-watching or taking photographs of animals he was able to put the war out of his mind. He found conferences very exacting, especially when, in the early stages, he had to face the ignorance, inexperience, stubbornness and arrogance of the Americans; at Casablanca, to counteract this, he would rise at daylight and go for a walk. It would delight him to find so many kinds of birds, white wagtails, stonechats and goldfinches, and on the seashore waders such as ring and grey plovers, sanderlings and turnstones. In places where he could not enjoy the relaxation of natural surroundings, he became overwhelmed by loneliness and a sense of emptiness. As an antidote to the war he invested in the forty-five volumes of Gould's *Birds*. He had wonderful value from them, not only because at the end of the war he sold them for twice the price, but because, during the war, Gould's wonderful pictures helped him to forget everything connected with it.

One may ask what made this man so serene, noble and magnanimous. There is no doubt that it was faith in God. He had complete assurance of divine guidance. As the evacuation of Dunkirk was completed, and at the blackest hour of the war, he wrote: 'I must say that it is very hard to see where we are heading for, but I have implicit faith in God.' Then a few weeks later, on being appointed Commander in Chief to repel the German invasion, he wrote to his wife: 'I find it very hard to realise fully the responsibility that I am assuming. I only pray God that I may be capable of carrying out the job. I know that you will be with me in praying God that He will give me the necessary strength and guidance.'

Two months later, when the Battle of Britain was at its height, he records: 'For the present there is nothing to be done but to trust God and to pray for His help and guidance.' Then, in October 1940, when the German invasion (Sea Lion) was postponed, he wrote: 'One can only thank God for the Providence that guards over one, and leave the matter in His hands.'

On the eve of the last great battle of the crossing of the Rhine, when he was discussing with Churchill the war struggle they had experienced together, he pointed out 'the part that the hand of God has taken at critical moments'.

Years earlier, when he was offered the post of CIGS, realizing the magnitude of the task, he wrote: 'I pray God from the very bottom of my heart that He may give me guidance and be at my side in the times I may have to go through.' It was at Chequers that Churchill took Brooke into his study and left him there to consider the appointment. As soon as he was alone, Brooke knelt down and prayed to God for guidance and support. Later he was able to say, 'I can now see clearly how well this prayer was answered.'

A great 'fighting man of faith'! Possibly, our greatest.

13

Sir John Laing, C.B.E.

Just as, in the Forces, we had leading men of faith who combined independence of thought with unfailing determination, so also in the civilian world there were men who stood out from among their fellows.

One such man was Sir John Laing, an exceptional person with a 'fighting faith', both in peace and war. His faith in God and righteousness led him repeatedly to 'launch out into the deep'. In his business life he demonstrated a true pioneering spirit. He applied modern scientific methods in the construction industry and introduced new ideas into his relationships with his work force. He was one of the first employers to give his employees the opportunity to become shareholders. He instituted holidays with pay in advance of other firms, pension schemes and bonus payments. Many of these new ideas later became standard practice in the construction industry.

He was associated with several major wartime engineering projects, for example the construction of Mulberry Harbour. The primary provision essential for the invasion of Europe was that of an area protected from the Atlantic waves where men and their equipment could be safely unloaded. In the First World War Churchill had put forward the idea of a breakwater for certain operations, and when the problems of open-beach unloading arose in the Second World War the idea was brought forward

again. This time Churchill was in command. Now the difficulties were not there to be argued about but to be overcome. So the famous prefabricated harbour, code-named 'Mulberry' was developed.

Great hollow ferro-concrete caissons, the size of five-storey buildings, were towed into position and sunk. Some 2,000,000 tons of preformed steel and concrete were moved across the channel and every available tug in Britain was used. Many even from as far away as America were requisitioned for this colossal towing operation. There were six miles of floating caissons and ten miles of floating concrete pontoons to be moved. The eventual harbour was twice the size of Dover harbour.

In spite of adverse weather conditions, during the first six days 326,000 men, 54,000 vehicles and 104,000 tons of stores were landed. By the end of three weeks 850,000 men, 149,000 vehicles and 670,000 tons of stores had been landed. In this operation John Laing played an important part.

His largest construction work during the Second World War was involved with the construction of airfields. This was exacting work and had to be done under conditions of extreme urgency. Altogether sixty-nine airfields were constructed. This involved a work force of hundreds, all of whom had to be housed and fed, and materials which had to be transported to some very remote areas. Every site had to be carefully surveyed for drainage, otherwise water would lie on the flat surfaces. Vast excavation work had to be undertaken. It meant a great deal of experimental work and personal supervision. John Laing regularly set out at 7 am to inspect sites. An air-ministry official declared that probably Laing's was the most conscientious and efficient company in the war involved in this kind of work. His own workforces were amazed at John Laing's energy, as at the age of sixty-five he continued to arrive early at the sites each morning and worked so hard and so thoroughly. Admiration was expressed for his personality and his leadership.

I came into close contact with John Laing during the Second World War and realized his greatness and his fighting faith. When we left Morocco we were allowed to bring out only a sum equivalent to £30. This meant that we arrived in England with no money and I telephone John Laing. He told me that he had a furnished house unoccupied in the Harrow area, which he loaned, rent free, to missionaries. He also gave me an interview for a job and sent his car to fetch me. He explained how his airfield contracts for the Ministry had mushroomed overnight and he offered me work. I did not feel that airfield construction was my line of work but I did feel that I might do well on the practical side. I moved to the north of England and joined Avro, now known as British Aerospace.

We spent some weeks at John Laing's house at Harrow. It is typical of the character of the man that, after we left, he found time, in the midst of all his war duties, to write a most interesting letter to me. We had brought the Anderson air raid shelter out of the garden, where it was wet and cold, and erected it in the sitting room over a double-bed. It gave protection from any collapse of the roof and flying glass, as well as being free from damp and cold. John Laing was highly intrigued with the idea and wished I had joined his firm as he would have been glad of a man with an adaptive and inventive nature. He also complimented us on leaving the house in better order than many others had done. Such praise was encouraging and heart warming in those difficult days.

Nothing ever seemed to be too much trouble for him and he was always kind and thoughtful. When I returned to London to take up work connected with MI6, MI9 and SOE, he would come across and speak to my senior Crusader Bible Class at Rickmansworth. This giving of his time was especially appreciated in the light of the important work he was doing in connection with the war.

After the war, one of his greatest achievements, and one which was of great personal interest to him, was the construction of Coventry cathedral. The old building had taken 125 years to complete and had been destroyed in one night in 1940. Using his best workmen, John Laing started work on the new cathedral in 1955 and the Consecration Service took place in May 1962, attended by HM Queen Elizabeth II.

Despite the scope of his business activities during and after the war, John Laing still found time for an amazing variety of Christian activities. He was at one time chairman of the Inter Varsity Fellowship and played a part in the establishment of Tyndale House. He was on the council of the Scripture Gift Mission and other interests included the Missions to Seamen and the Royal National Mission to Deep Sea Fishermen.

He was also involved in movements for the benefit of deprived children such as the Müller Homes in Bristol, the work of the Dr. Barnado's homes and Fegan's Agricultural Schools.

But his vision went far beyond his own country. He travelled abroad, giving both encouragement and practical financial support to overseas missionaries. This involvement in the work of foreign missions led him to contribute generously to the work of the Bible Society.

It was in the production of the colloquial Arab Bible that John Laing played a part which was of particular interest to me. Captain E. G. Fisk, after serving for many years in Morocco, was faced in 1952 with the possibility of missionaries being turned out of the country. He decided that in such an event it was essential that the people should have a translation of the *whole* Bible. There were immense difficulties, not only in the translation but also in publication and finance. Fisk received both encouragement and a generous gift from John Laing. After a visit to Morocco in 1966 I called on Sir John, then over ninety years of age, and told him of the continuation of the work. On this visit Sir John showed me, with some pride, the copy of Fisk's Bible which had been presented to him by the Bible Society. He was also responsible for the establishment of a Bible Depot in India, the Bible House in Harare and the internal reconstruction of the Society's headquarters in London.

Although he was involved in so much great work, both secular and spiritual, and although he came into contact with the nation's leaders, John Laing remained a humble man and lived a life of greatest simplicity. He was in truth a saint who did not withdraw from the hurly burly of ordinary life into seclusion. He had a great capacity for enjoyment and a deep appreciation of the simple and beautiful things of the natural world.

One secret of his greatness was that behind his quiet and pleasant manner lay a strong will and a determination not to compromise where integrity and high moral standards were concerned. He was a man who built his life on the sure foundation of faith. Like Abraham, the father of faith, John Laing also looked forward to the abode which God has designed and built, the dwelling place with permanent foundations which is eternal in the heavens. At the age of ninety-nine, John Laing, architect and builder, took up permanent residence there.

He had never been interested in amassing a personal fortune. Instead he had given away millions of pounds to charitable movements, evangelical and missionary work, Christian youth groups and church building. When he died he was worth only £356. It was a striking testimony to the way in which he had practised the faith which he professed.

14

The Common Connection

The men about whom this book has been written were different from each other in many ways; yet they shared one thing in common – their faith in God. Like us, these men knew the meaning of fear. How then did they seem to be so fearless when faced with problems and dangers? In every case it was because of their confidence in God and in his Son.

In the serving of a righteous cause, faith is of ultimate importance. It is more important than the preservation of one's life. Danger and death can be faced with acceptance and without fear when we know that only the body can be killed, and not the soul. Jesus Christ himself said, 'Fear not men, who can only kill the body.' He taught his followers that God alone was to be feared. And it was Jesus who warned his followers, 'In this world you will have trouble'; but he had already promised them, 'In me you may have peace.' He had also promised them freedom; 'If the Son sets you free, you shall be free indeed.' When we fear God, then other fears can be overcome. It is only the Christian who can live a full and fearless life of liberty – liberty of mind and soul.

Three thousand years ago, this was the experience of David, an Old Testament 'fighting man of faith'. Again and again he faced danger and death, but his poems, the psalms, show us that the person who fears and trusts God is not afraid and is truly free.

Today we are still involved in warfare. We are surrounded by evil. Some of it is the work of a minority given over to such evil. They use all means, including that of the media, to try to drag others into their own cess-pool. The Bible teaches us that as individuals and collectively we are engaged in a continual fight against evil.

Again and again ordinary warfare is used to illustrate spiritual warfare. Paul, the veteran New Testament warrior of faith, gives various instructions to Timothy about this warfare. He expresses the hope 'that inspired by them you may wage the good warfare, holding on to faith and a good conscience'. Elsewhere he exhorts this young man to 'fight the good fight of faith'.

The writer of the letter to the Hebrews stirs our hearts as he recalls the faith in God of men and women over a period of two thousand years. He writes, 'They . . . through faith . . . conquered. They became mighty in war . . . put aggressors to flight . . . and enforced justice.'

Daniel rose to be Prime Minister in the mighty Babylonian kingdom. Speaking about deceitful rulers who win support from all who abandon religion and justice, he declared that those who truly follow God will fight back. He sums up the situation in these words: 'People who know God shall stand firm and do exploits.'

The whole of life is a battlefield. Nehemiah, who in 445 BC was rebuilding the walls of Jersusalem with a band of helpers, records that 'each kept his weapon to hand'. Of the spiritual warfare, Paul writes that we are to be armed with 'the whole armour of God, so that when evil comes you can stand your guard'.

Any army or individual who is inadequately equipped will suffer defeat. Paul emphasizes that it is the *whole* armour of God that we need. In Ephesians 6 he uses a series of pictures drawn from the complete armour worn by the Roman soldier as he went into action.

The *belt* around his waist – truth. What could be greater than this?

His *breastplate* – righteousness. Integrity is something worth aiming at.

His *shield* – faith. This shield provides a defence against all attacks of evil.

His *sword* – the Word of God. A sword is a weapon for attack. When Jesus Christ was attacked by Satan he answered with the words, 'It is written . . . you shall not'.

His *helmet* – salvation. Through Christ we have salvation from the guilt and judgment of sin. Through him we have also salvation from the daily power and domination of sin. In this way our 'helmet of salvation' protects us.

No wonder Paul could say, 'Thanks be to God who gives us this victory through Jesus Christ'. May we know the victory which comes from using the whole armour with which God supplies us!

The lives and deeds of the men whose stories are told in this book can provide inspiration and the encouragement to resist evil of all kinds which surrounds us today.

Yet they too had faults and failings. Though they were great men, none of them would have denied that there was still much in their own lives against which battles had to be fought.

But they claimed to follow One of whom that could not be said. If we are to fully understand the achievements and the character of these men, we must consider the Master they served. So we need to look more closely at the one who was without fault, the man above all men, the master of every situation, Jesus Christ. He was not only perfect man, but perfect God. The life that he lived showed his deity. Paul stated, right at the beginning of his letter to the Romans, that Jesus was 'declared with power to be the Son of God by his resurrection from the dead'.

It was this resurrection that vindicated his claim to deity and set the seal upon his substitutionary sacrifice. 'He was made sin for us, who knew no sin.' Because he was sinless he was the only one who could die for man's sin and win him forgiveness. 'In him we have redemption through his blood – the forgiveness of sins.'

The New Testament gives us a wonderful picture of Christ both as perfect man and 'in the fulness of his godhead'. We do not need an artist or sculptor whose effort to portray Christ in paint or stone limit him to his human aspect. The only portrait we need is the glorious vision in the New Testament, of the Christ who is both truly God and truly man. Peter was able to say, 'We were eye-witnesses of his majesty.' So we, with spiritual sight, can see his sovereign splendour in the Scriptures.

I often think of what Churchill said to Montgomery concerning the greatness of Christ. Montgomery interested Churchill more than any other general, and his visits helped to brighten Churchill's closing days on earth. Once Monty asked Churchill to define certain great men. As he did so, Churchill discovered that they had great failures as well as great successes. When Monty asked Churchill about the greatest among religious leaders, he gave a very simple and interesting answer. 'Christ's greatness was unequalled, his death to save sinners unsurpassed, his sermon on the mount the last word in ethics.'

Although many great leaders never acknowledged

the lordship of Christ in their own lives, they still testified to his supreme greatness. We need to acknowledge him as both Saviour and Lord. That is what these men of faith we have been considering did.

So too did Peter Churchill, one of our leading SOE agents. In a book about his captivity, *In the Hands of the Gestapo,* he speaks of his newfound faith, gained by reading the New Testament. He writes:

> The battle of faith required scars before it was won. Despite my best endeavours and prayers, control of myself would slip through my fingers with exasperating ease, until I fully realized that God was doing everything possible to help me pass the waiting time with patience and in peace of mind.
>
> With the possibility of execution at any moment, I was calmly able to accept that the gate of death is but an entrance to the real life hereafter.

Peter Churchill believed in the one who said, 'I am the resurrection and the life'. He was able to say with Paul, 'Death is swallowed up in victory'.

John Newton had been a notorious and cruel slave trader before his conversion. Afterwards he could write:

> Why should I fear the darkest hour,
> Or tremble at the tempter's power?
> Jesus vouchsafes to be my tower.
>
> Though hot the fight, why quit the field?
> Why must I either fly or yield,
> Since Jesus is my mighty shield?
>
> Against me earth and hell combine;
> But on my side is power divine;
> Jesus is all, and He is mine.

Pilot Officer Barton was awarded a posthumous

Victoria Cross. I wish I knew his full story, so that I could close this book with it. His life was so short that perhaps such a story would not even fill this page. Yet his last words to his mother are the greatest anyone could write.

> Except for leaving you, I am quite prepared to die. Death holds no fears for me because I have trusted Christ as my Saviour. All that I am anxious about is that you and the rest of the family will come to know him.

In this, he echoed the great desire of the apostle John in his Gospel. 'These things are written so that you may *believe* that Jesus is the Christ, the Son of God, and that believing you may have *life* in his name'. (Italics mine.)

Many of the outstanding men of the Second World War were men who were grounded in the Word of God, and whom he had been preparing for such a time.

It is my hope that this book has introduced some of them to a wider audience.

Abbreviations

ADC	Aide-de-camp
CB	Companion of the Order of the Bath
CBE	Companion of the Order of the British Empire
CIGS	Chief of Imperial General Staff
CMG	Companion of the Order of St. Michael & St. George
CT6	'Comforts for Troops' (Officially Clothing & Textiles 6)
DSC	Distinguished Service Cross
DSO	Distinguished Service Order
GCB	(Knight) Grand Cross of the Bath
GCMG	(Knight) Grand Cross of the Order of St. Michael & St. George
GC	George Cross
GCVO	(Knight) Grand Cross of the (Royal) Victorian Order
GHQ	General Headquarters
GOC	General Officer Commanding
GSO 1 or 2	General Staff Officer 1 or 2
KBE	Knight Commander of the Order of the British Empire
KCB	Knight Commander of the Bath
KCMG	Knight Commander of the Order of St. Michael & St. George
KG	Knight of the Order of the Garter
LLB	Bachelor of Laws
MC	Military Cross
MI6	Military Intelligence (Espionage etc.)
MI9	Allied POW escaping, evading and life lines, interrogation
MOS	Ministry of Supply
NAAFI	Navy, Army and Air Force Institutes
OBE	Officer of the Order of the British Empire
OM	Order of Merit
OSS	The earlier American equivalent of today's CIA (Central Intelligence Agency) the USA counterpart of MI6

PIP	Preservation, Identification and Packaging of stores
SAS	Special Air Service
SASRA	Soldiers' & Airmens' Scripture Readers' Association
SNS	Special Night Squads
SOE	Special Operations Executive